JOURNEY *of the* HEART
Reflections on Life's Way

JOURNEY *of the* HEART
Reflections on Life's Way

GERHARD E. FROST

Compiled and Edited by Naomi Frost

Augsburg
MINNEAPOLIS

JOURNEY OF THE HEART
Reflections on Life's Way

Scripture quotations are from the New Revised Standard Version of the Bible,
copyright © 1989 by the Division of Christian Education of the National
Council of the Churches of Christ in the USA and used by permission.

Credit lines and permission acknowledgments for previously published material
can be found on pages 127 and 128.

Cover design: Tara Christopherson
Cover photo: David L. Hansen

Library of Congress Cataloging-in-Publication Data
Frost, Gerhard E.
    Journey of the heart: reflections on life's way / by Gerhard E. Frost.
    p.   cm.
    ISBN 0-8066-2829-4
    1. Meditations. 2. Spiritual life–Christianity. 3. Frost, Gerhard E. I. Title.
BV4832.2.F753   1995
242—dc20   95-8356
                                                                         CIP

The paper used in this publication meets the minimum requirements of American
Standard for Information Sciences—Permanence of Paper for Printed Library
Materials, ANSI Z329.48-1984.   ∞

Manufactured in the U.S.A.   AF 9-2829

99   98   97   2   3   4   5   6   7   8   9   10

Contents

Foreword

"I have entered a large and strange room," Gerhard Frost, my father, told a church group during his last year of life as he approached seventy-eight. "It's called 'aging'."

"I don't know anything from past experience about what that room contains," he continued. "I once was a very little child. That helps me to understand very small children. I once was an adolescent, and then a young adult. Of each stage I can say, 'I was there; I've been through it.' And it does help to understand. But I've never been old. I cannot see into my life through any previous experience. I live on a frontier every day. I am an explorer, and it's scary."

I suppose every stage of life is experienced as a frontier because each is new to the person living it. But the later stages may be at once more rewarding, a product of years of personal investment and accumulated insights, and also—as Dad found—scary, a time when certain abilities are deteriorating, not developing, and one's peer pool steadily evaporates.

Journey of the Heart offers reflections on my father's inward journeying, spanning forty-plus years of his writing, approximately the latter half of his life.

I can't say of Dad what is so often said of people entering and passing middle age, that he "mellowed." He'd always been mellow. He had a way of looking at things from all sides, respect for an opposing point of view, and the imagination to don others' shoes and walk a few of their steps. He had the gift of being a good listener and being open to another's reality. But I think he became more at ease, in his later years, with the intersection of others' experience of reality with his own differences. He came to enjoy this frontier of discovery.

In a chapel talk excerpted in this book but addressed to college students in the 1940s, my father declared—I picture him with youthful vigor and a full head of hair—his need for "a Voice which says things that do not need to be revised." Some 30 years later he confesses in these pages, "as I grow older I find I have fewer certainties and need fewer."

I believe that Dad never stopped listening for the Voice that would guide his journeying. I think he heard with his heart its ever deepening revelations.

—*Naomi Frost*

LONGING

I Am Resolved

I, who teach,
am resolved never to forget
that I am of the journeying people of God.
Therefore I will love answers,
but I will love questions more.
I will not seek docile acquiescence,
but suffer the creative struggle.

I will remember
that our wilderness has no terminals,
only trails,
that truth is not a static destination
toward which I journey
and at which I arrive.
Rather, it is a horizon:
I never exhaust it,
but as I journey
I have the journeying person's great reward,
a larger world.

—from "A Second Look"

Roses in Winter

I am writing these lines on a perfect summer day. Just outside our door three rosebushes are in full bloom. Their velvet petals will soon fall to the ground. Their fleeting fragrance will be lost on the summer breezes. But we will remember. God gifts us with memory so that we may meet our best moments again and again. As someone has said, "God has given us memory so that we may have roses in winter."

The truly Christian memory is adept at forgetting what needs to be forgotten and remembering what needs to be remembered. It can sort through the remembrances of a lifetime, tossing out the bad, saving the good. It can discriminate.

We sometimes regret our inability to remember, but we often ignore our failure to forget. When we fail to forgive, we retain memories that become intolerable baggage on the inward journey. When we cling to resentments and jealousies, we cripple ourselves with increasing bitterness. Whenever we refuse to let go of the trivial, we sap our strength for shouldering what's essential.

Forgiveness is a beautiful form of forgetfulness. This absentmindedness is heaven-sent. As we grow in age and in grace, we should remember that persons suffer more depression and despair because they can't forgive and forget than because they can't remember.

When our hearts are gripped with hopelessness or homesickness, it is good to have something great to look back on. It is good to have something to remember. Memories can do much to steady us in our moments of stress. Our inward and forward journeys are best pursued if we can be nourished by rich and rewarding memories. But it is tragic to live in the past to such a degree that we walk backward into the future.

We live in expectation. We look forward, as we remember. This is the habit of the Christian, for this is the meaning of the life of faith.

—Portions from "This Land of Leaving" and "Chapel Time"

Journeying

Journeying begins with leaving. We leave the womb for this larger world and call it birth. We leave the home of our childhood and call it growing up. We pass through the middle years and enter old age. We leave the earthly home and call it death.

Always there is pain in leaving, the pain of leaving and of being left. But there is also joy, for without leaving there can be no arriving. We welcome the first cry of a baby, not because we like to hear a baby cry but because its cry signals a successful transplanting from the pre-natal to the post-natal environment.

As God's journeying people, we sometimes are driven by changing circumstances and other times are drawn by our own yearnings.

There are journeys of the feet, the geographical journeys in which we must leave the familiar for the unfamiliar. Most painful among them is leaving one home to build a new.

There are journeys of the mind. These are often threatening. Great courage is required when I am asked to let go of old prejudices or faulty judgments. To change my patterns of thinking and responding is difficult. They seem to be a part of my very bone marrow and bloodstream.

Then there are journeys of the heart. These are concerned with my loves and loyalties. Only God can free me to forsake the trivial and devote myself to the best. Only God can draw me into a deepening relationship and a greater commitment to God's dream for me.

I think now of moments when I have faced helplessness, or times when I have been forced to reconsider a course of action in which I have invested my very self. Such occasions are the essence of the inward journey. They tell us that the time has come to change before we reach the point of no return, to take a new look at what God wants us to become.

Life's journeys are challenge all the way. They must have their weaning moments. To make terms with moving on, we first must leave behind some cherished baggage. Then we can continue our journey as God has intended. The person God wants each of us to be is our permanent business. Our hearts keep telling us this; yet we are prone to weed every garden but our own, neglecting to keep house in our own inner chambers.

Do we cling too long to a person or an experience or a place or a dream? We may make ourselves too dependent on loved ones, refusing to let them have lives of their own. We may refuse to live in any place but where we are. By refusing to adjust or adapt, we may be committing gradual suicide or causing untold damage to those we love.

For me and for you, the journey from sunrise to sunrise means letting God's Spirit heighten our aspirations and hopes, broaden our sympathies and understandings, and widen the horizons of our thought and activity. It is to let the Spirit make us more truly what God knows we can be.

—*Portions from "This Land of Leaving," "Chapel Time"*
and "Deep in December"

My Longings

What are my actual wants—not my whims, but my needs? I want to feel that living has a truly great reason. I want abiding assurance that days are meaningful, that life has a worthy destination, a dependable Guide, and a sure direction. I want something to do and an adequate reason for doing it. I want to hear a voice which says things which do not need to be revised.

I want to be true. I want to be honest. I want to be consistent. I want to be able to pray "thy kingdom come" and "thy will be done" without feeling that I am but a kneeling lie. I want to live with my conscience as I read my Bible.

I want my children to be safe. I want to be happy. I want to be healthy.

I need Christ. Without him there is no significance in my present task and no anchor for my future trial. Without him I choke on every prayer and lift my eyes to a vacant sky.

I want a song, a song that is inspired by an event, that makes an eternal difference, a song that is true. I want this song to sing, but I also want it to give.

Lord, I can never compose this song. Give me a song, I pray.

And then, dear Lord, I want a star to follow, something to look up to.

A savior, a song, and a star—these are my vital needs, and this is my prayer.

—*from "A Savior, a Song and a Star"*

God's Longing

Any consideration of human longings—the hungers of the heart—must begin with God's expressed longing for us, the people, and his created world. The safest place in which to think about our complex, elusive moods and feelings is in the love of God.

God reads you and me. God sees our restless search for joy where there is nothing that lasts, our hectic chase after material possessions which can only be lost, our self-defeating effort to find fulfillment where nothing can fully satisfy. Our creator asks whether we want to be forever free and fulfilled.

It is one thing to say that God has created all that exists and quite another to confess with Martin Luther that "God has created me." The moment I affirm that God has created me I no longer belong to myself. I'm not intended to live my life as the main character in my history. I give up my "right" to myself. I become a steward. I am set aside for new responsibility and godly concern. At this moment, too, I find myself in relation to right and wrong patterns of life investment, for I encounter a purpose against which to measure my thoughts and acts.

But God is faithful, so we need not be crushed by life. When we feel defeated, we may trust Christ in defiance of our feelings. It was not for failure that God created us.

God always takes the initiative. You and I have never prayed a prayer in which our word was the first word. The first word in our prayers is the presence and person of God, God seeking and we responding. The Hound of Heaven is always on our trail, and once he has found me, once he has found you, he continues to seek us on deeper levels than we have permitted him to find us.

This is a gracious cycle. The more he seeks, the more we, by his grace, respond.

Today I will not think of taking Jesus into my little life but rather of letting him take me into his. My limited vision and dream are swallowed up in the vast dimensions of his life, death, and resurrection. As he lives and reigns to all eternity, I shall ever live and reign with him. Staggering thought! But this is God's promise.

—*Portions from "Hungers of the Heart"*

Why?

We are God's question-asking creatures. This is a part of our essential dignity. We are meant to ask. We thirst for meaning, and each answer leads into a deeper question.

We sometimes think that we lack only the answers. The truth is that we lack even the right questions. But God turns the discussion in the right direction when we come to him, regardless of what we are wise enough to ask.

Faith is not destroyed by inquiry; it is fed. God has not given us the capacity to ask questions with the purpose of driving us away from him but of drawing us closer. When questions are asked in the spirit of humility, they do not destroy mystery or damage faith. They enlarge our world of knowledge and cause us to sense more deeply the mysteries around and within us.

A Christian educator has reminded us that "the proper place for mystery is at the end of the inquiry, not as a substitute for it. If there does not seem to be much mystery in life for you, it is most likely because you have given up the inquiry too soon."

Our questions take many forms: Who am I? Where have I come from? Where am I going? What am I intended to do along my way? These and many others, but the most painful question is: Why? Why is there so much loneliness and pain in the world? Why is sin permitted to run so far and be so fierce? Why did my child die?

It is not wrong to ask why. It is necessary. But there are many ways of asking it. It can be snarled. It can be cursed. And it can be prayed.

Faith's celebrations do not put an end to questions. Rather, they change the mood in which questions are asked.

Sometimes we want to ask even when we know the answer. We need the assurance that comes with having our knowledge confirmed. And yet there are occasions too when we are afraid of the implications of our knowledge.

It is good to lift our "why?" up to God in the spirit of prayer, holding it before him as a child holds an empty cup up to its mother or father for filling to the extent of need. God's wisdom and love will give answers sufficient for our capacities. Too much knowledge would crush us; too little would starve us. God knows us. He understands our questions and invites us to ask.

A comforting promise envelopes each one of us: "The Spirit of truth . . . will guide you into all the truth" (John 16:13). This does not mean that as followers of Christ we will always know as much or see as far as we would wish, but it does mean that God will take our hand. Our Father will see that his child is not deserted nor left without the Spirit's witness in a strange and difficult world.

The hunger for certainty is with us all, but as I grow old I have fewer certainties, and need fewer. I can only describe my inner life by saying that I bow before its mystery. And life is simpler now.

The word still holds: "Blessed are those who have not seen and yet have come to believe" (John 20:29).

—Portions from "Hungers of the Heart"

Those Strong Feet

I fled Him, down the nights and down the days;
I fled Him down the arches of the years . . .
I hid from Him, . . . from those strong feet
that followed, followed after . . . .
          —Francis Thompson

We are the questing ones, we say,
searching, groping for our God.
But would that we could know ourselves
as he knows us—
fugitives, escapees, rebels,
the wanted ones, the longed-for ones.

God is the questing one,
the gaunt and tireless one;
he calls and sends us to one another
to speak the wooing Word, the Name,
to break each habit of ingenious evasion,
and gently block all exits
from chastening love,
to listen for each footfall of those strong feet
that even now follow, follow after.

—from "A Second Look"

Attics

There's something about attics
that can mesmerize and paralyze.
They're good for tripping,
and forgetting this present world.
It's best not to risk a visit to the attic
unless one is prepared to let twenty minutes
become half a day.

The "I remember" room,
it brings lumps to the throat
or chuckles of recollection.
With half a century for forgetting
I smell our attic yet,
and see it, too.
Seed corn drying by the chimney,
National Geographics piled against the wall,
sentimental throwaways that just wouldn't be thrown,
and things outgrown or out of date.

One needs to visit the attic of the heart,
the musty, back spaces of the mind,
to bring to remembrance the days
when one clung to too small a God
and confessed an inadequate creed,
too cramped for the human situation.

It is well that we visit our attics,
but, as Mother used to say,
"Don't drag things down."

There's beauty and deep meaning in the attic,
but it mustn't be the living room.
It's not for changing,
just remembering,
And to live is always to change.

—from "Bless My Growing"

Journeying Through Prayer

We never grow up to—much less outgrow—the privilege and promise of Christian prayer, but we do outgrow some of the prayers themselves.

By nature we ask for pickles and jam, for three-car garages and three-layer cakes. We try to turn prayer into a kind of grab bag and complaint counter. We ask in order that we may consume God's gifts for our own purposes.

Who among us hasn't at some time passionately pursued a mistaken goal or fallen in love with a potential disaster? Life's journey means leaving for the purpose of arriving at a new place: Among the things we leave behind are certain of our prayers.

Sometimes our prayers are empty forms and nothing more. Then they work as a deadly anesthetic to our spiritual life and growth.

The devil enjoys a religious parade. He likes to see you and me in it if he can lock step with us and if it can be confined to flag-waving and lip-service. Our adversary stands ready to offer hush money to any conscience that will settle for high-sounding phrases, dressed in their Sunday best but kept at a comfortable distance from life.

We need the comfort of knowing that prayer does not consist in poise and eloquence. Honest need does not stand on dignity. A hurt little child flings himself into the arms of the one whom he believes will hear and receive him. She blurts out her need, sometimes with sobs that make her speech unintelligible. They trust the other to understand.

There is a boldness that does not come slowly or hesitantly to Jesus. It rushes at him and clings to him. It refuses to be driven away or put off until another time. It claims what it needs. And this boldness gives joy to our savior, for it is born of trust. We are invited to come boldly to the throne of grace.

I cherish an incident my older sister relates concerning our father. When she was a very small child she came to him and said, "Papa, I have a problem. I need to talk to you." Our father replied, "What is your problem?" And the child said, "I always fall asleep while I'm saying my prayers." And he answered, "Well, is there a better way of falling asleep?"

This story tells me much about my father, and even more about my Father, God. Surely, my father's advice to my sister didn't mean that we should wait for fatigue to overtake our prayers and let that suffice for our relationship with God. Instead, it showed sleep as the ultimate act of trust.

We cannot explain our predicament, but Jesus does not require this. His understanding runs ahead of our prayer. And he knows that even the strongest among us is just a cry for help.

Other times our prayers take the shape of words and express themselves in more or less articulate phrases. But the soul and essence of prayer is a cry, the wordless cry for all that we know we are meant to be. It is a cry for God, and it finds its answer in Christ.

—Portions from "Homing in the Presence"

Looking with a Child's Eyes

Simeon blessed God and said, "Master, now you are dismissing your servant in peace, according to your word; for my eyes have seen your salvation, which you have prepared in the presence of all peoples" (Luke 2:28-31).

Some years ago, when we had a small son in our family circle and it was his turn to select the hymn for our family worship, he would most frequently choose "The Battle Hymn of the Republic." From the time he was about seven until he was eleven or twelve this was his favorite choice. Somehow he had been moved by this song, and his imagination must have called forth visions of great goodness marching victoriously against every force of evil.

Just yesterday another child's imagination caught me up. I was with a group of adults waiting for dinner, enjoying a relaxing conversation but listening also to a six-year-old's running commentary on the subject of dinosaurs. He was drawing a picture for us as he talked of meat-eaters, plant-eaters, and other interesting facts he'd learned. All the while, he continued drawing his picture.

When he had finished, he showed it to each of us in turn. We all praised the picture with its two dinosaurs against a detailed scenic background. The young artist received our compliments with dignity and pleasure, and then said calmly, "And there's a lake that doesn't show."

A lake that doesn't show. The child has eyes for the invisible! He lives in his unfettered imagination and frolics there. He makes happy use of a gift that most of us have shelved as unworthy of adult behavior.

Imagination is more than a playground for the mind; it's the banquet table of the heart, food for the soul, and a vital source of strength and energy for our daily struggles.

Often our hearts may be full of anxieties that drown out the Spirit's message of peace and power. What if I lose my health? What if inflation eats up my dollar? What if she won't marry me? What if he doesn't love me any more? Without the eyes to discern it, there can be food for the soul with no soul for the food.

The kingdom of God is here, even when we can't see it clearly. Our manner of life will either sharpen or obscure its presence. We affirm an invisible kingdom where God is at work and where wonderful things happen. We who believe owe this vision to others.

Happy are they who can join with that child and affirm that their eyes have indeed seen the glory of the coming of the Lord.

—*Portions from "Homing in the Presence" and "Silent Spaces"*

Time

Every new year brings one which some of us will not finish. We measure time because we have so little of it and because we know that we live in the ever-present possibility of sudden interruption.

"What time is it?" Stranger asks stranger. All of us mortals are peculiarly united by the clock.

"Today's trouble is enough for today (Matthew 6:34)," Jesus has said. One day at a time. Today's grace is more than sufficient for today's trouble.

I remember a charming little blonde I met one evening in the front pew of a church. As I sat beside her I fell back on the stock question with which adults bore little children: "How old are you?" She answered, "Seven." Since I had a seven-year-old in my own home at the time, I made a remark to the effect that there were many things that one could do and how much fun it was to be seven. She agreed, but then added wistfully, "But I keep thinking of nine!"

I don't know why this child happened to think of nine, but I do know that she was giving voice to a universal human characteristic, to project ourselves into the future. Other times we become stuck in the past. Faithless focus on tomorrow, or vain regret over yesterday—either way we lose the present. Both consume vital strength for the struggles of living.

When we reach into the future and anticipate everything that may happen, we add an imaginary weight to that which we already carry. Add this to yesterday's burden, and it crushes even the strongest. To try to live tomorrow before it is today is like holding a weight at arm's length. Even an empty hand soon becomes intolerably heavy when held in such a position.

It is natural to look at the face of the clock, but we need to remember that there are some things that it can't tell us. It can tell us that the time is 6:53 or 12:25, but it can't tell us time's meaning.

Christ teaches us to receive the day as gift and challenge, remembering his all-sufficient grace. To the believer time is a gift of love from him who alone can give it. Every moment is his moment. His compassion and power go with it.

Grace is given in pace with need. I am not strong enough today for tomorrow. Tomorrow is another day, and God's grace will be new and sufficient for it. God's mercies are greater than our experiences of them. Therefore today need never be the measure of tomorrow.

"Teach me, O God, not to torture myself, not to make a martyr out of myself through stifling reflection, but rather teach me to breathe deeply in faith." This prayer of Søren Kierkegaard strikes the note of abundance. Jesus doesn't keep us just barely alive. He does not intend that we shall live by gasps and gulps, dragging ourselves around with no energy for living beyond ourselves. Rather, he provides for abundant living, the kind of living that has time and strength for others.

If you and I could walk with Jesus for a day, we would find him taking time to place his hand on the head of a frightened child; time to restore purity to a woman like the one at Jacob's well; time to touch the white scabs of a leper and send him on his way rejoicing; time to take the wild look out of the eyes of a lunatic; time to teach a priceless lesson to the veriest simpleton; time to hang a new star in the spiritual horizon of a Nicodemus.

Everything ticks if only we will listen. No moment is meaningless for one who lives in relation to Christ. God's purpose is being worked out for each one of us in the sure movement of the days and weeks and months and years.

Each moment is meant to be redeemed. To redeem is to invest, to put something into the moments as they pass. Time is redeemed when it is filled with love. For each of us, life is just long enough to cast our ballot, to say our "amen" in acts of love and concern and so affirm in this way that God is good.

What time is it now? Is it early, or is it late? It is always early since Christ makes all things new. And yet it is always late, for we are totally dependent on him.

Perhaps the ticktocks of our clocks are the footfalls of our seeking God as he comes in countless ways, offering new opportunities to give—and to live!

What time is it? Time to turn to Christ in faith, time to lift one's eyes in hope and trust, time to stretch both mind and heart in prayer and praise.

—*Portions from "These Things I Remember" and "Silent Spaces"*

Perpetual Surprise

I'll not forget that hot August day
when I stopped for a Coke
and got pentecost.

I, a very young pastor,
two months in my parish,
hot and thirsty
from walking from house to house,
felt it.
I sensed in my very soul
what I'd never experienced so deeply before
and seldom so dramatically since:
the Almighty Father
really cares for me
and all his people;
he's "got the whole world
in his hands!"

Can it be that grace takes us by surprise
in the midst of the ordinary and the repeated?
Why shouldn't this be so,
because grace is from outside us,
not within?
It is God's interruption,
his wonderful invitation.

Grace is God at his unpredictable best.
No vision of Christ duplicates another,
for love defies the stereotype.
To believe is to live in perpetual surprise
and expectation.

—from "Bless My Growing"

Silent Things

I like to think of silent things:
sunbeams and stars,
meadows and mountains,
rocks and fields,
and especially winding paths.

Silent happenings—
like dawn breaking
and evening coming on,
summer fading into autumn,
April deferring to May,
planted seed
and truth well taught—
silent things that won't be forced
and can't be hurried.

God's Spirit broods
over silent things,
movements of life
and ministries of love.

There is healing in thinking
of silent things.

—from "Blessed Is the Ordinary"

Lord, I Believe

"Lord, if you choose, you can make me clean" (Matthew 8:2).

"My daughter has just died; but come and lay your hand on her, and she will live" (Matthew 9:18).

Two confessions of faith: one from a lonely leper, the other from an anxious father, but both saying the same thing: "Lord, you are in command."

What is faith? The books can't really tell us, but we can see it in those who believe. When I meet a person who seems strangely tall because he has bent low, one who is bold because she has a big God, one who keeps going on when every circumstance would say to quit, one whose life affirms that God is in command—then I may be assured that I am glimpsing the life of one who has faith.

At some point the first man had to say to himself, "I am a leper." It must have been a hard moment. We wonder, did he always have hope? Or did he hear of Jesus and then hope revived? Whenever or however hope may have come to him, the important thing is that he now had it and acted upon it. He "came to him beseeching Jesus, and kneeling said to him, 'If you will, you can make me clean.'"

"Clean"—what a brave word for a leper! The man had been dead to his society. He had been forced out of all that he most enjoyed and lived for. He had been required to keep his legal distance. Now everything would be different. The man who had been dead would be able to return to his life and loves.

Jesus responded. Moved with pity, he stretched out his hand and touched him, saying, "Do choose." In the second incident, another picture of beauty and power is before us. A ruler forgets his position and comes as a father. He who is accustomed to showing authority bends his knees. He whose habit is to command comes with a prayer.

"My daughter has just died; but come." Faith refuses to let death have the last word. It does not surrender to death's false finality. It will not let this last enemy have its way.

"And Jesus got up and followed him" (Matthew 9:19). What a surprising and comforting discovery, that he who asks of us that we follow him, responds to our cries and follows our needs!

God's word of power is still with us. Wherever hope is set on Christ, that word takes effect. God still honors his word.

Are you downcast? Do you feel unclean, unloved, and lost? Has the crushing weight of life become too much? Then set your hope on Christ and expect compassion. Hope and ask. He will not shame you. He will not send you away empty-hearted. Our faith is God's work, as yet unfinished.

I'm Afraid

God, I'm afraid,
afraid to pray,
"Thy will be done."
I reach for a hard hat,
expect my sky to fall.
I almost hold my breath.

I know your will is more than best;
it is the only good.
Forgive my deep distrust,
the sin I've sinned
and sin again.

Remove the dark suspicion
from my heart.

—*from "A Second Look"*

Keep Me Restless

Hand in hand we walked and talked
as we climbed the winding stair
(she was only three)
in the big house.
I tempered my giant stride,
enjoying every moment.

"What are we doing?" she asked.
"Looking for my car keys," I replied.
"Oh, Granddaddy," she exclaimed,
"you're always looking for and
looking for!"

"The story of my life," I said,
but only to myself;
she couldn't have understood.

But, Lord, you understand.
I'm yours, I'm of your searching clan,
at home away from home.
Lord, hold me, steady my faltering steps,
but keep me restless in my rest,
waiting, hoping, journeying,
"always looking for and looking for."

—*from "Kept Moments"*

Bless My Growing

Lord, I've been wondering:

Why do I say I?
Why must I ask why?
Why is joy so close to pain?
Why do I feel transparent in the presence
of a child?
Why am I often lonely in a crowd?
Why are people so sober before a clock?
And a ten-dollar bill?
Why am I so loud when I'm wrong?
Or so fierce when I'm afraid?
Why is the human face most beautiful
when it is looking up?
Why, in moments of crisis,
do people either curse or pray?
Why does prosperity drive us apart?
And adversity bring us together?
Why is it painful to celebrate alone?
Why does my ability to ask questions
exceed my capacity to receive answers?
Why am I a mystery even to myself?

Lord, give me the right questions,
and bless my growing.

—from "Bless My Growing"

FOLLOWING

Christ's Question

Jesus asked his disciples, "But who do you say that I am?" (Mark 8:29).

An earlier question had been more comfortable: "Who do people say that I am?" (Mark 8:27). It permitted each listener to remain just a face in the crowd. It was like watching heat lightning on a summer night. But this—"But who do you say that I am?"—was like having lightning strike a heartbeat away.

Life's journey is single file. As Martin Luther said, "Everyone has to do his own believing, just as everyone has to do his own dying." It is great to join with others in the Confession of Faith, but in the moment of being questioned, the first word must be "I" not "we," for I cannot speak for you, and you cannot testify for me for the affirmation of what we believe when we find ourselves in God's presence. Soon or later, one stands before the Lord. Not with parents, family, friends or humanity in general—all alone, alone with the big question—this is my life situation and yours.

Faith in Christ does not let me be a spectator. It makes me a participant in the event of my salvation.

After we have reached the highest goals of education and piled question upon question, always stretching ourselves to refine and sharpen our inquiry, God's question remains: "What do you think of Christ?" This question provides the permanent horizon within which we live. It is before the beginning of time, and yet it is as new as this morning's sun and as right as rain.

What do I think of Christ? My answer today will not be quite the same as yesterday. For as my experience of his grace lengthens in time, it deepens too, and yesterday's answer grows. God's question is not meant to taunt or torment us but to coax and invite us along the path of deepening peace and joy.

Nativity

I visited my friend today.
He's eighty-five
and travels light,
a wise and wonderful man.

We spoke of many things,
small talk and big talk,
and then he said,
"Yes, for most of our
comings and goings
maps are OK,
but for the Big Trip
we still follow the Star!"

Thanks to you, elder brother,
wanderer in my wilderness,
man of faith and vision.
You keep Christmas
in my heart.

—*from "Kept Moments"*

Follow Me

"Jesus saw a man called Matthew sitting at the tax booth; and he said to him, 'Follow me'"(Matthew 9:9).

Our God is a promise-making and promise-keeping God. He has committed himself to us and rescued us. Now we are summoned to live in the light of that rescue.

The kept promises of God shape the life of each believer into a promise to keep. Because He has come, I must go. Because God has found, I must seek. Because God loves, I too love.

Whether you're eight or eighty, the call is still Follow me. Jesus calls us to a challenge continually new. To follow him is to participate, not just to observe; to get involved in new experiences and responsibilities.

Søren Kierkegaard has said, "It is hard to believe because it is so hard to obey." By nature, we climb as high as we can go. We scramble to achieve. We covet the place of power. But grace invites us to climb down. Instead of struggling toward the top, to live in lonely isolation, we are invited to lowly places of new responsibility and concern.

God makes every virtue real. Our way is to write a book, 300 pages on humility, 350 on service, and surely 700 on love; then present it in five volumes to the publishers, collect the royalties, be proud of the work, hate every competitor, and die of jealousy the first time that someone writes a better one. God's way is to make an apron of a towel, kneel on kingly knees before a Judas, wash feet that are at home in life's deepest gutters, and demonstrate enough love in twenty minutes to exhaust the combined life spans of puny persons. While we find the highest places and the loudest trumpets God stoops down to the lowest sin, serves his way through the humblest ministry, a bloody cross, a silent grave, and up to the brightness of eternal day.

We all think of ourselves. It is as natural as breathing, and it is not necessarily bad. But I need to think things through in terms of God's gift to me. I need to remember that I am not called by Christ to compete. I am not expected to take another's place but to find my own.

One cannot follow without leaving something behind. By God's daily grace we seek to leave yesterday's person behind in order to become more and more fully what the Holy Spirit would have us be. Our only competition is with ourself, our yesterday's self.

Whenever I ask, "What do I get out of it?" I am looking at life upside-down. When Christ gives himself to me in forgiveness his next gift is something and someone to give myself to. He knows that one of my very first needs is to throw myself away like seed cast into the ground. I need to get the weight of myself off my hands.

Pride misses the majesty of life because it either rejects God or makes of him a last resort. To humble oneself is to make God one's first resort. It is to explore life in terms of God's intention rather than to try to force one's own conception of achievement. In short, it is profound liberation.

When Jesus says, "Follow me," he offers me the freedom of the integrated life; he gives me himself in a loving fellowship which involves me in worthy causes and offers channels for all of my energies.

To believe is to give your life for what you believe, not usually in one great moment of exceptional heroism, but more often in small moments of tiring and draining effort. Drop by drop, through the years we pour our blood into what we really believe. We spell out our creed in each little, hidden deed. We grow old, applying what we know to what we are really committed to, and in the end, no one who has lived with us needs to ask what we stood for. It is all clear.

To stand at the foot of Christ's cross is to shoulder new responsibilities or intensify old ones. To stand in his presence will always mean to accept concerns which may surely be evaded by the simple, but tragic, expedient of refusing to stand there.

For most of us, God's command doesn't take us away from what we are presently doing. It fills our lives with new significance by reordering our priorities and requiring us to submit our activities and plans to the test of Christian concern and love.

Tomorrow will be another of God's Mondays. People will rouse themselves to get back into the harness. The commuter traffic will be heavy in every city. Today, and tomorrow too, there is Jesus. He inhabits the next moment, filling it with explosive potential. He calls me, not to desert my work, but to transcend it by making it his. Tomorrow, as today, if we listen we will hear him say, "Follow me."

—Portions from "A Savior, a Song and a Star"
and "Deep in December"

Go and Do

"But be doers of the word, and not merely hearers who deceive themselves" (James 1:22).

It is damning to know, if one does not then go and do. Truth, unapplied, becomes the lie one tells oneself. This is a lie that can kill. Truth is meant to happen!

Jesus tells us that an honest person acts on what he knows. Procrastination, the lag between the good we know how to do and know we ought to do and the length of time it takes us to do it, is a dishonesty. To temporize when we are called to act is a universal sin.

How many people have bled or starved to death while we, the Christian church, were quoting scripture? It is convenient to take things into consideration, to deliberate but not decide, to listen but not act. It's fine to quote scripture if we work while we talk. Otherwise, we had best keep still.

We look for our King. We want him to come. And we pray, "Thy kingdom come!" But when he comes, he comes most often unrecognized, for he comes clothed in need.

That frightened child, that forgotten old woman, that socially rejected criminal, that dispossessed ghetto youth, that lonely alcoholic, that hollow-eyed beggar, that tattered tramp, that empty-souled high spender, that bored and fed-up playboy, that work-worshiping drudge —the down-and-out and the up-and out—I met them all today on my street, and in them I met my King.

There is sadness in every "it might have been," in every song unsung or every good word unsaid. The unlived moments of our lives are those in which we reject the ones who need us, the moments when we pass by our King.

I hear about love. I read about it. I talk about it. I see posters, listen to songs, watch movies about love. Gradually I begin to think myself a loving person. But in reality I have only heard about it. I don't really care. I am an actor.

Jesus says: Let it happen! Begin where you are and follow where love leads. It will take you into pain and peril, but you will be real. You will not be living a lie.

God gives his gifts freely, to be freely shared. "We have gifts that differ" (Romans 12:6). There is no question as to whether we have them. The question is, will we use them or lose them?

Let no one say, "There is nothing I can do." No one has to make his or her life count; it already does.

As Jesus once sent his disciples, so you and I are sent. We may go in many ways. It may be by the miracle of our money. It may be in prayer support if we are bound to a place of helplessness, if we are aged or infirm. It may be by packing our essential belongings and leaving where we are, or it may be by staying at home. More than likely, it will be all of these ways and many more. Where there is a burden that needs lifting, each one of us is either freight or power.

Inaction leads to inner hardness. "Won't" becomes "can't." Failing to right our social wrongs and seek justice, while talking of love, we dry up the inner resources of our community and our individual selves.

God has already acted and waits for our response. He would not say, "Go," if he himself had not come. Jesus is still saying, "Go and do!"

Called to Remembrance

I remember meeting one of my former students at the doorway of a city church. It was on Good Friday. He was holding two handsome little boys by the hand, one on either side of him. I remarked that he was in good company, to which he confided, as an aside to me, "Yes, that's true. But this little fellow to my right wasn't happy when he had to put away his toys and get dressed for church today. He wondered why we had to go to church on Friday. I explained to him that this is the day when we remember that Jesus was crucified for us. And he said, 'But I remember it.'"

In this child's comment we sense the different ways in which the word "remember" may be used. To remember may only be to note a fact as fact and stash it away on a high shelf of the mind. But this is not remembrance. True remembrance is contemplation, meditation, and assimilation. It is the process by which an event takes hold of my life and yours and becomes a formative factor in our living and the very texture of our days.

When we deceive ourselves into thinking that remembering means reciting or lecturing, we lose sight of the fact that remembering really means receiving. When we remember Jesus, we are shaped and sustained, nourished and formed by him. We feed our expectations on our faith in him. We grow because of God's gracious activity within us. We sense a bigger and bigger God, and are able to accept and respond to him, to trust him more and more.

Remembering is more than an intellectual experience; it is a total response. As we Christians remember Jesus together, we share each other's gifts. By defining ourselves in terms of our common expectations and memories, we reinforce the fact that we belong to the same family and are of the same body; the body of Christ, risen from the dead.

When our Lord said, "Do this in remembrance of me" (Luke 22:19), he asked that we place ourselves before his face, that we exteriorize ourselves before him and offer ourselves to him for cleansing and revision. He leaves no depth of our experience untouched.

—*from "These Things I Remember" and "Homing in the Presence"*

Our Father

I prayed today,
prayed "Our Father."
An airport was my cathedral,
the busy one at Newark,
the crowded one in New Jersey.

I didn't fold my hands;
I didn't close my eyes
or bow my head.
I looked straight at them,
I looked at God through them—
through my brothers and sisters.

I looked at "our Father"
through his hurrying,
hoping, trying, crying
family.

He looked right back at me
and smiled.

—from "Bless My Growing"

The Perfect Prayer

The Lord's Prayer is the perfect prayer, perfect in proportion, unclouded in its spiritual direction, unselfish in its central ambition, unconfused as to ultimate destination. It gives balance and stability to our own personal prayers.

From birth to death, from the font to the grave, The Lord's Prayer is with us. It is a part of us in times of crises, in times of tranquillity, in times of upheaval, in times of quiet growth. It is with us in the moving shadow time of the day and in the bright sunshine of life.

It reflects Christian joy and privilege, breathes a spirit of reverence and godly fear, and is completely within God's will.

It is, itself, an answer to prayer. The disciples prayed, "Lord teach us to pray." This is the answer they received:

Our Father, who art in heaven . . .

My God is not a distant, indifferent force, but a present and personal God who parents and feeds his children in Christ. According to St. Augustine, the name "Father Almighty" suggests that our creator, who sustains all things, is "God in power" and "father in goodness." What a combination! Earthly parents are sadly limited in both love and power. In God these are united, and whoever hallows God's name receives that love and power into their lives.

I doubt that we are to think only of maleness when we say the name, "Father." I think we are to bring together all the best that we've ever seen or experienced of human caring.

Hallowed be thy name.

God's name is his lifeline thrown out to drowning persons. It is his point of contact with each one of us in our need.

What does it mean to hallow God's name? Martin Luther says: "when the Word of God is taught in its truth and purity and we, as God's children, lead holy lives in accordance with it."

The answer seems commonplace. It has a Monday sound; it suggests breathing exercises to the vocalist or finger drills to the pianist. We would prefer something more spectacular. It reminds us of obedience.

Thy kingdom come.

To join with others in calling God "our Father" is to respond to the Spirit's work in the secret places of the heart. To pray "thy kingdom come" is to look for ways of spending the family inheritance, ways of giving ourselves to family tasks and concerns. Thus invited, the Holy Spirit makes timid and hesitant disciples bold with the courage of being accepted by Christ and made joint heirs of everything in God's kingdom.

This prayer is for more than passive patience. It is for grace and power—for strenuous Christian living. This prayer is the believer's way of rolling up his or her sleeves to tackle the kingdom task.

Thy will be done on earth as it is in heaven.

"Thy will be done," we say, and brace ourselves for disaster. "Thy will be done," we pray, and grit our teeth for some new pain. Why must we pray these words as though it is our Father's joy to see us suffer?

What is the will of God for us? It is that you and I shall express what he had in mind when he gave us life. It is that we shall live in a relationship of believing, receiving, and serving.

Give us this day our daily bread.

God's name, God's kingdom, God's will, and a good brown loaf of bread. What a divine combination! The God whom we have come to know in Jesus Christ as "Father" considers the body no small thing. He is vitally concerned with grocery lists. But he wants our prayers to be more.

There is a pledge implied in the words, "this day"—a pledge that I'll be back tomorrow. I'm that same pesky little kid who bothered you yesterday. I'm here today and I'll be back for tomorrow's forgiveness, and on the way I will forgive.

Forgive us our trespasses, as we forgive those who trespass against us.

The Lord's Prayer moves from bread to forgiveness. This is right, for while bread can sustain our existence only forgiveness can turn existence into life. A person with a full dinner plate may still have an empty heart.

We ask much when we ask bread but infinitely more when we ask forgiveness. The miracle of the loaf of bread is as nothing when compared with the miracle of grace.

Christ is the living bread, "the bread of life from heaven to weary pilgrims given." We bemoan the high cost of living; how often do we give thought to the price of life, our Lord himself?

Lead us not into temptation.

To invite temptation is wrong. To encounter it is inevitable. This petition is not a prayer for immunity or exemption from the tests and trials that are inherent in our existence. We know that there are no safety zones in which we may live in spiritual ease. Rather, this is our prayer for the whole armor of God so that we can face and defeat the enemies that surround us. So fortified, we go out into the dangerous streets and run the errands of each day.

But deliver us from evil.

This prayer runs ahead of us and follows after us. It not only includes present deliverance and release from our past; it takes the longest possible look into the future.

Beyond the immediate to the ultimate, beyond the momentary to the eternal, the wings of this petition carry us straight to the lap of our Father.

For thine is the kingdom, and the power, and the glory, for ever and ever. Amen.

Although this doxology is not found in the ancient manuscripts, it has become accepted by many as the church's response to its Lord in the praying of the Lord's Prayer. It is essentially a confession of faith, an expression of self-surrender.

We fight the good fight as those who are already on the winning side. The victory is not in doubt because Christ has won.

The Lord's Prayer has so much of the universal in it that it stays ahead of us all our lives. Each time we come to it we receive more, not because it has changed but because we have. As a classic, it respects our readiness and meets us at whatever point we are in our inward journey.

Can it be that life's journeying is made meaningful, not by pay raises and possessions, nor novelties and sensations, but by Lord's Prayers sincerely prayed, benedictions truly received and appointments with our faithful Father carefully kept?

Opening to Surprise

I am aware that I walk in "the valley of the shadow." But I believe that I am also called to "walk in the light." Death looks over my shoulder, but life walks by my side. This means that I am to be a great expectant. My mind shall be set on receiving what God gives and filling each moment with good. I am to look forward, not backward. I am to walk and run, not hide.

God comes to me in infinitely various ways, always bringing new gifts. Life from his hand is perpetual surprise. A favorite seems to be liberating truth, one of those wonderful "I see!" moments when life is enlarged and enhanced.

We never know what form the goodness of God may take. Grace is an untamable, unpredictable factor in each day's events. Pentecost tells us that God is not only around; he is involved with us. He trips us up just when we are stepping high with our own proud plans and purposes. Or he lifts us up just when we are flattened out with disappointment and despair.

God's comings are occurring constantly. Sometimes they happen in the stillness of the night when no one else is present. Sometimes God comes in the noise of the factory, other times in the stillness of the cathedral. He walks in the dawn and the dusk, in the night and in the day. He cries out in the midst of injustices; he whispers to us in our pain. He invites us in our pleasures; he rushes at us in the mighty winds of new desires.

Most often God's comings happen through other persons, gestures of kindness, smiles of friendliness, acts of love. Sometimes he comes in a look or the touch of a hand, or a little child's kiss or question, other times in the turbulence of a frightening experience; sometimes in a "chance" meeting or in a sentence in a book.

God comes in ever changing circumstances, events that turn distress into pleasure, and restlessness into peace and a sense of well-being. Always, when he comes, he comes for us and to us. God wants all that we are.

I hear much today about being assertive, too little about being open. Because I can't pursue the best but am pursued by it, I am called to be prepared to let God's promptings become my welcome guests. And so my travels are a continuing journey in the light into greater light.

—*Portions from "This Land of Leaving"*

Blessed Is He

John, the faithful forerunner and fearless preacher of Christ, found himself living with his lonely thoughts in Herod's prison. Day after day, night after night, fierce questions surrounded him like beasts in a jungle stalking their prey. Finally he shaped his tortuous question and sent it by messenger to Jesus: "Are you he who is to come, or shall we look for another?" The question is stark and honest. It expresses the depth of John's doubt.

We all know something about Herod's prison, the dark moments when we have no feeling of peace. Then we too ask, "Shall we look for another?" This happens even to one who has known the Lord for a long time and has served him faithfully.

In our daily journeying as well, much of our restless striving is really a matter of facing away from Christ and "looking for another." Most of our mistakes consist in waiting for things and people already here.

I counted the years until I could go to college. But I didn't really "go to college" when I got there. I wasted study time and cut too many classes. Opportunities for education were all around me, but I waited for another.

I was lonely and needed a friend. But with people all around me, I didn't show myself friendly. I didn't reach out to that person who stood ready to be kind and loyal. I waited for another.

I saw an opportunity to speak courage into a frightened adolescent, but I "looked for another." I was asked to stand up and be counted in an unpopular cause, but I "looked for another." I was invited to partake of the pain and deep pleasure of loving in an unlovely and unlovable world, but I "looked for another."

So much human regret lies in recognizing opportunity too late!

"Blessed is anyone who takes no offense at me," Jesus said in answer to John's question from prison. There is a certain sternness and severity in the reminder Jesus gave to John the Baptist. It tells us that one may look for the wrong things even when one looks at Jesus. One may be mistaken in regard to the meaning of his mission.

John had been sent to run interference for Jesus, Mary's child. He was to prepare for, and usher in, the new. The child John had become a mighty man, strong in the strength of the Sender, single minded, and committed to his task. Like a lighted candle his life was spent. Freely he gave of all that he was. Fiercely he contested with evil. Courageously he challenged the entrenched powers in their corruption and tyranny.

As Jesus became more and more, John became less and less. Then one day he died—died under the flash of an executioner's sword, died at the command of a drunken king to fulfill the desire of his hateful wife. But Jesus called him the greatest of men.

They had named him John and had asked, "What shall this child be?" Only God knew. God knew that John would be great, great in faithfulness. And blessed was he.

We Are Witnesses

"Soon afterwards [Jesus] went to a town called Nain, and his disciples and a large crowd went with him. As he approached the gate of the town, a man who had died was being carried out. He was his mother's only son, and she was a widow; and with her was a large crowd from the town. When the Lord saw her, he had compassion for her and said to her, 'Do not weep.' Then he came forward and touched the bier, and the bearers stood still. And he said, 'Young man, I say to you, rise!' The dead man sat up and began to speak. . . . Fear seized all of them" (Luke 7:11-17).

Many things can happen to parties. A dinner party may need to be postponed because the guests don't arrive. A birthday celebration may find the honored guest too ill to attend. A wedding may suffer last-minute cancellation because the bride and groom have experienced a change of heart or mind. But a funeral is a funeral, and nothing much can happen, because the central character is dead.

On this day, however, the unheard of happened. There was a meeting, a meeting between Jesus and death. Enemies met, and Jesus was the stronger.

So it was on Easter as well. Heaven sent its Best, and the world gave him its worst. But this crucifixion didn't become just another among many horror stories. This crucified one didn't seek our pity or defense, much less our patronage. He bids for our hearts, our trust, our worship. His cross represents the battle before the victory. It is the price of redemption and possession, the atonement bridging separation and alienation. History's cruelest day became forever "good."

Because we live at the cost of Christ's life, we can never again take life for granted or forget how blessed we are. In him we see all deaths conquered, for he is the strongest of the strong. In him our hopes meet and unite.

To confess one's faith is to gather one's gifts, the better to consider them and rejoice. Today let's gather our gifts: the forgiveness of sins, the resurrection of the body, and the life everlasting. Let's see them in their newness.

Then the time comes to take these gifts into the streets and put them to use. As servants of Christ we are called to be faithful stewards of the Gospel by breaking the despairing and deathly silence of estrangement and self-will with the good news that God forgives. We dare not keep secret what God has made known.

Recently I sat at a table outside a place where many people come, a well-known hamburger stand, advertising so many billion sold. I watched as I ate, and I thought about myself and my brothers and sisters who came and went. I asked: What is perhaps the most prevalent problem of the masses of people today, myself included? I found myself saying: To find an adequate purpose in daily living, one that can offer significance and dignity. To find a shaper of dreams, a motivating presence. To find God.

Sharing in Christ's resurrection gives me release for all the pent-up power for goodness that I have ever known.

We float the increasing cargo of meaning, the gathering variety of burdens and excitements that make up our lives, on this one great central event, this second creation of our God. God has recreated and renewed my life and yours in the risen Christ.

We are to be witnesses, Jesus tells us. People can serve as witnesses when they have seen something happen to another. But we are more authentic witnesses when we can say it happened to us. So it is with our witness for Christ. We need to be able to say that the resurrection has happened to us, that Christ lives in our hearts, that he walks with us and upholds us.

Jesus is here, we proclaim. Our alleluias can be shouts of relief from the settling dust of boredom that covers so many lives. Come, join the parade. Come to the party, if you would know joyous sobriety and sober joy.

Give Thanks

"I give thanks to my God always for you because of the grace of God that has been given you in Christ Jesus" (1 Corinthians 1:4).

The love of one believer for other believers breaks out in the winsome words of Paul when he says, "I give thanks to God always for you." It is an expression prompted by the grace of God.

The Holy Spirit has one special purpose for you and me, to bring us to faith in Christ, to lead us to the place of affirmation and praise.

Coming together in worship, we celebrate the fact of belonging. We live in a continuing Pentecost. There may be no visible tongues of fire nor sound of rushing wind as there was on that first Pentecost, but there will be a quickening of the impulse to love. There will be a new sharing in the Father's plans and purposes.

It can be hard on the ego to rejoice with those who rejoice. To enter into another person's celebration without envy is a gift of grace, especially if we ourselves have not already held that particular celebration.

Praise—given to God for God or to God for other persons—expresses the health of the praise-giver. It needs no command for it is the spontaneous response of faith to the saving fact of Jesus Christ.

"Therefore I will praise thee," says the psalmist. Praise must be deeply personal before it can blend into the unison sound of many voices. I must have a very big "therefore" or my praise will trail off into an echo of despair.

Faith in Christ spells itself out in as many different ways as there are people. Since our gifts differ, so does our witness, for our witness is shaped by our gifts. One man will express his faith in the work of his hands, another in the eloquence of speech. One woman will find her fulfillment in loving involvement with her children, another in a more public career. The young person will speak praise in one way, the aged person in another. Even the very little child will find a way to be heard. Yes, there are many kinds of witness, but all say the same essential thing: Jesus is Lord. We give thanks.

Be Ready

"Be prepared," they told us
when we were very young.
"One must always be ready for death.
We live in the valley of the shadow;
don't be taken by surprise!"

They meant to teach us well.

But what of the other half?
"Be prepared for life.
At any moment it may assault you.
Be ready for the sudden storms of truth.
Listen for the thunder, and watch for the lightning
that plays along life's horizons.
Be ready for the crashing break-in
of an overpowering meaning or an all-consuming love.
Our enemy, death, broods and hovers, 'tis true,
but over all towers our taller friend.
He awaits his moment too.
Expect to be surprised;
there's always new welcoming to do."

—*Adapted from "A Second Look"*

Share the Party

Jesus said, "Go therefore into the main streets, and invite everyone you find to the wedding banquet" (Matthew 22:9).

"Go to the main streets," Jesus says. But does he really mean the freeways of New York and Los Angeles? Does he include the rush-hour traffic of our busiest city streets? Or is this the language of a peaceful little parable in a slow and sleepy day?

The day and the command are ours. The church is a fellowship that is drawn to God but at the same time is thrust into the maelstrom of human living. We are not meant to isolate ourselves from one another or to insulate ourselves against another's need. We are to be open. We are not asked to select. It is for us to bring them in. "Everyone you find"—what could be simpler than that?

God has no favorites. This is a hard lesson for us to learn. Most of us were reared within protective walls, fenced in by provincial attitudes. We had favorite places and people, special customs to bind us to our families and communities. These ties were good and necessary, especially when we were very young, in order that we should feel secure. But our very securities can become our prisons.

God is not fenced in. He "is generous to all who call upon him" (Romans 12:12). We dare not exclude when God has included all. We are not the keepers of the Door.

If God were just instead of merciful, we would be destroyed. The good news is that history is the story of him who says: I choose to give. "I choose to give myself. I send you my Son. I choose to give him to you and for you. And I choose you as my very own. But I choose others too. You must not try to be my only child. Take pleasure in my goodness to others. Rejoice in my impartial mercy and in my free choice to save instead of to condemn."

The banquet hall of salvation has not changed. It is well prepared. Its doors are all open, the guest list still unlimited. Our ministry is to invite.

Air and light and water are for "everyone you find." They are universal needs. Christ is such a need, though often denied. He meets us as the universal one, the one without whom we cannot live. Name, age, sex, race, or other condition—all are insignificant. The Spirit cuts through the red tape and addresses us all, but one by one.

Deeper than any craving for food or drink lies the hunger for fulfillment and meaning, for well-being and dignity. It is the basic longing, the hunger for restored humanity.

We want to be what we were meant to be. We sense that we are not now all that we are intended to be. We live with a nameless sorrow. It is the anguish of the unlived life, of imprisoned goodness, of lost righteousness.

Yes, the whole world is one in hunger. It is also meant to be one at the banquet table of grace. We who call upon Christ's name are to break the barren silence around us and give voice and hands and feet to him who is and ever shall be God's living Word.

Who can resist celebration? It is the church's most convincing witness. If we are true to the resurrection, the world will begin by peeking through the cracks and listening at the windows; then one by one believers will be drawn to the open door.

If the church will be what it really is—or, rather, if you and I will be the church—God will find a voice through us that his saving will be known to "as many as we find."

—*Portions from "These Things I Remember"*

Don't Laugh

They told me today
of the chain smoker who read so much
about the hazards of smoking
he decided to give up reading.
They expected me to laugh.
And I did.

But then I thought,
"What about me?"

Our Lord says,
Love one another,
love your enemies,
seek justice,
forgive as you have been forgiven.

Something in me doesn't like that.
So sometimes I read less
and less.

Don't laugh.

—from "A Second Look"

Make Me More Impulsive

I see taillights, Lord,
taillights of opportunity
vanishing into the night of yesterday;
I've watched them through the years,
tormented by the story I am
but haven't often shared:
the "little Christ" I'm called to be
but haven't always been.

I've played it oh-so-safe, Lord,
picked my careful, plodding course.
Make me more impulsive,
more prodigal for you.

—from "A Second Look"

LOVING

Do Love

Is there a big enough "do" to swallow up and contain every "don't"? There is no motivation in "don'ts."

The answer is "love," responsible Christian love. Love moves us to love.

I am meant for love. God has sent me to cross bridges to the hopes and sorrows of others. When Jesus speaks the ancient command, "You shall not kill," we can't think only of blood on the hand. It goes much deeper. Thoughtless gestures, spoken or unspoken insults, loveless or indifferent attitudes—these can become bloodless atrocities against the hopes and dreams of my brothers and sisters, acts that can stifle the spirit.

The commandments, "You shall not kill, You shall not steal, You shall not covet, You shall not commit adultery" are summed up in one "you shall": "You shall love your neighbor as yourself."

Love is the capacity to get into other people's skins. It is the readiness to see through other people's eyes by putting oneself in another's place. Love's first work is to listen. Until one has heard, one cannot speak authentically or hopefully. To love one another is to want to know one another. It is to have patience to listen. The greatest loss a human being can suffer is the loss of the capacity to love.

Love is not squeamish. It means business. It takes off its cloak and rolls up its sleeves. It applies its whole will to its task. It takes pains. Love not only means business; it knows its business. It keeps in practice. "We love because he first loved us" (1 John 4:19).

Self-service leaves neither time nor energy for loving. Nothing is so preoccupying as sin, nothing so tormenting as envy. And nothing is so wearying and wasting as self-protection.

Love makes toddlers of us all, because we are ever trying to grow up to it, always learning, often failing. God has no grown-up children here on earth when it comes to loving. These are all in heaven.

"God is love" (1 John 4:16). We are silenced before so vast a truth, silenced as by a starlit sky on a cloudless night. God is love, and in Christ we witness perfect love. Perfect love's first work was to die, to set its own plans and wishes aside and take the hard road. So it was on Calvary.

Perfect Love bends very low; it stoops to cleanse sinners; it girds itself to serve traitors. It is not jealous of its own rights. It is not a devotee of convenience. It counts no opportunity an interruption.

"God so loved the world"—and the world must know through you and me this great good news.

But no unbeliever can be argued into believing in the gospel. God is not found at the end of an argument. God is often found by one who has been invited to "taste and see that the Lord is good" (Psalm 34:8).

—Portions from "A Savior, a Song and a Star"

Rhythm and Relating

Jesus was as public as a water fountain, yet as private as Mount Everest. He penetrated deeply into life on our streets, yet withdrew fully from the noise of our world. He knew and lived in the necessary rhythm of togetherness and separateness.

A rich private life supports a contributing public life. In all human living, rhythm is essential. When we tamper with this rhythm, we lose the balance which is necessary to well-being.

Life is a matter of routine and repetition, an unbroken succession of little things. But the so-called little things aren't little at all. They are the minutes, the hours, the days through which we grow, change and become. They are the essence of human living.

God gives his greatest gifts in little things. He doesn't arrange his world for the giraffes among us. He makes ample provision for his little people, leaving some cookies on the bottom shelf. One of these daily blessings is the gift of family, friends, and neighbors. In respecting and enjoying those who live closest to us we experience some of our best God-given moments.

My hand is meant to fold into yours. Your word of friendship and approval can feed me when I'm hungry and pick me up when I'm tired. Your careful word of reproof may warn me of impending danger. A look or smile, embrace or gesture, exchanged with you in an alien place, may give me new heart and courage for living.

Among the most compelling of our longings is our hunger for intimacy. This hunger draws us into the joys and risks of relationships.

Relationships are sustained by communication. The most inclusive of relationships is that of friend to friend. In fact, friendship is the real substance of every significant relationship. Jesus once called us friends, and in so doing gave us our permanent vocation as friend-makers. Even marriage and family can have no real intimacy without friendship. It is a fact that many husbands and wives, many parents and children, many siblings, aren't friends! Too many relationships are closed against intimacy for lack of communication and response.

Friendship means living through changes together. When we walk and talk together, we imprint our thoughts and concerns on one another. We shape each other. We help each other to change and grow.

The "I remember" moments increase like ripening fruit hanging heavy on the vine, blending the strength and sweetness of the vanished seasons. When the sun begins to set on my life's day, I am sure that I will see that some of the best time I ever invested was that time I gave to being a friend.

Solitude and fellowship, silence and conversation, rest and work—these are significant contrasts in our life's experience. Silence is good when it is balanced by conversation. Our Lord Jesus Christ didn't draw apart in order to become a hermit or to desert his task. When he sought the quiet places, he did so in order to draw strength for the crowded ones. Self-discovery may require radical loneliness. But it is also true that we cannot fulfill ourselves, or experience our true destiny, if we remain withdrawn and aloof.

Day and night, high tide and low tide, summer and winter, spring and fall, systole and diastole, inhale and exhale—all of these suggest that balance is necessary to life and growth. For the spiritual journey too, there must be quiet times alone with the Spirit and active participation in the press of the crowd.

—*Portions from "These Things I Remember," "Hungers of the Heart," "Deep in December" and "This Land of Leaving"*

No Regret

In the long catalog of regrets,
one I've never heard
and don't expect to hear:
a dying person saying,
"If only I hadn't given so much!"

—from "Kept Moments"

I've Begun Asking

I'm breaking my habit
of asking strangers,
"What do you do?"
as if they're no more than what they do.

I've begun asking,
"What are your dreams and your dreads?
What moves you, excites you, alarms you?
What drains you or sustains you?
What interests or bores you, amuses or grieves you?
Where do you go when you're homesick?
Where do you rest when you're tired?
Who are you when you're alone, and whom do you miss?
And who misses you?"

But when we're dealing with questions,
perhaps it's really not what
or where
or who,
but whose.
Whose are you?
And whose am I?

—from "A Second Look"

Judge Not

"Be merciful. . . . Judge not!" Jesus said.

Of course, we must "judge" from moment to moment and from day to day. Life is an unbroken chain of decisions and choices. But Jesus is not speaking of the moral judgments and fine distinctions which we are called upon to make. He is not referring to the constant encounter with issues before which we must say yes or no. He is talking about our judgments against people, our pronouncements of their unworthiness. When we judge our fellow humans, we depart from mercy; we cut the life-line from our heavenly Father to ourselves. We forsake Christ and put aside his saving work.

When I meet a person, I immediately begin appraising him. I enter into the dangerous process of making distinctions, many of which are neither important nor good. I remember an aged Christian giving this advice long ago: "Practice prayer rather than appraisal." It is good counsel.

The Christian faith is not first a program of ethical uplift. It is rather a growing sensitivity to forgiveness.

Some years ago I heard a lecturer say, "No person is ever to be merely tolerated." I was startled. I had heard people, good people, talk about tolerance—racial tolerance, religious tolerance, other varieties of tolerance. They implied it was a generous and Christ-like attitude. Today I see tolerance as a dirty word.

I know now that mere tolerance is a cruel and inhuman attitude, a woefully inadequate expression of the gospel of reconciliation. How do you like to be tolerated, like a plumbing fixture or a window frame? To strike a person may be less dehumanizing—at least it is to see him.

Jesus tells about two men who went into a temple to worship. One lived by rules and carried a ruler. He was hard on himself, but he felt like an insider; he was a great deal harder on outsiders. He lived his legalistic life and spent himself in "trying harder" to maintain the high position he was sure he must hold in his Maker's eyes. He congratulated himself and God.

The other man left his ruler at home. He didn't feel like an insider, but he had an inconsolable longing. He hardly dared look at himself;

it made him so sure that he deserved to be an outsider. He knew he wasn't much at praying, so he just threw himself at God's mercy. One man asked nothing and received just that. The other asked much and received more. "I tell you," Jesus says, "this man went down to his home justified" (Luke 18:14).

Peace is the choicest fruit of pardon. It can only follow forgiveness. Where there is guilt, there is no peace. This peace is God's answer to the conflict that passes all human understanding, our own enmity against our holy and righteous Creator.

Judgment destroys the judge. Nothing is more destructive of human resources than playing God. He has neither called nor equipped us for absolute judgment. We can't "bring to light the things now hidden in darkness." We can't know the secrets which a righteous judge must know.

In order to judge we must be perfect in love as well as justice, and we are insufficient in both. When we judge another, we commit a greater sin than any we can presume to judge. Therefore, we dare not judge either the servant or his or her service. Our only safe course is to be on our own errand and leave the judgment to God.

—*Portions from "These Things I Remember"*

Where Is He Now?

Time has passed, but I can't forget
one nameless face.

I saw him for most of a year—
at least three times a week—
as I waited for Jersey buses
in New York's 167th Street station.
Almost always he stumbled
along the waiting line,
extending a grimy and unsteady hand.

But this day was different,
a Sunday in late spring,
the station deserted except for three,
the man, my wife, and me.
Less disheveled, more at peace,
he didn't beg, but sat serenely
in the unused shoeshine chair.

A woman entered, perhaps a grandmother,
with a comely child in springtime dress.
To our surprise, she turned and said,
"Please watch her while I telephone."

We watched the child by the telephone booth;
I watched him, too,
the man in the shoeshine chair,
saw his lips move as he talked to himself
and gazed at the waiting one.
Then, fumbling in his pocket
for a cherished treasure,
he drew it forth, a very special thing—
a rosary.

Hesitantly, tentatively, he approached her,
the wee one waiting unafraid.
He placed his offering about her neck,
then, with high ceremony
and deep contentment,
he resumed his place in the chair.

Why did he do it? I've asked myself
through passing years; where is he now?
Who was he, that derelict on 167th Street?
Was he—is he—a saint, I wonder,
nearer than many who scorned him
to the Kingdom of God's grace?

—from "Blessed Is the Ordinary"

Forgive and Forgive

"Lord, if another member of the church sins against me, how often should I forgive? As many as seven times?" (Matthew 18:21).

Peter was conscientious. Like all careful people he wanted things to be black and white. He liked things neat. So he asked the practical question, as if to say: Let's get this straight right from the start. How often shall I forgive the person who sins against me? What is expected of me? How many absolutions to a person? In other words, when can I quit?

The answer came back: You can't.

Forgiveness has nothing to do with the measurable or the calculable. Mercy does not add or multiply; nor has it to do with science, exact or otherwise. Mercy is heaven's art.

To live in God's forgiveness is to live out forgiveness. To refuse to forgive is to refuse to be forgiven. But to be forgiven is to enter into the celebration of God's mercy.

In a world of hatred and enmity the natural response to one who attacks is to attack in return. One blow calls for two. A hard blow calls for a harder. And so conflict increases and hostility feeds on hostility.

To "get even," to "settle it once and for all," to "put her in her place" by matching hatred with hatred and force with force serves neither justice nor love and in the end destroys.

There is a Christian way to take the offensive. The way of Christ is to fight evil with good. Remembering Jesus Christ as we face each other in the midst of disagreements and heated encounters helps us to begin to see each other through his eyes. It means we will listen as he would listen, giving ourselves in costly attention. Reconciling love generates itself.

In his Sermon on the Mount, Jesus tells us reconciliation is the first in the order of business in the Christian life. When harsh words have been spoken and someone has slammed the door, we may be tempted to leave it that way. But Jesus says: Stop. Find your hurting brother or sister.

I want to turn a deaf ear to this. I am frightened where feelings are involved, mine as well as the other's. I want to answer, "But he was the offender" or "But I can't make it right with her." I want to prove my rightness or explain my wrongness. But Jesus has the last and best word: "You are my disciple. You have me. You are rich in relationship, and it is all on account of grace. Now, since I am your door to blessing, open all doors."

It is both the pleasure and pain of old age that we see and hear everything more multidimensionally than we once did. This is why it is so hurtful when aged people quarrel. So much insinuation and innuendo, so much potential for pain! History hides in each word and look and gesture.

Nothing is more burdensome over a life's journey than to refuse to let go of a hurt or an insult, or to refuse to forgive or accept forgiveness when forgiveness is called for.

But age can also be an asset in relating to others, because we experience everything in greater depth, and more as a whole, than we did when we were young. Our accumulated knowledge and deepened self-understanding can make us more mellow and merciful as well as more discerning and insightful. With memory that spans generations we can, when we want to, be most reconciling and healing in our later years.

Don't burn yourself out in hot resentment and don't waste yourself in cold contempt. Rather, in all your important relationships, let this be the season of golden harvest of love and understanding.

When can we quit forgiving? Only when God does.

—*Portions from "Deep in December"*

Marriage: a Joyful and Fearful Thing

The life of faith is a life of freedom within the boundaries of love
and in the context of responsibility. By faith we celebrate Christ and
the salvation which he has brought. But this celebration overflows
into celebration of persons. For the Christian, it is involved in every
human relationship.

In marriage two people enjoy each other as persons. They cherish
each other's differences and complement each other. They express this
through communication in many forms, but especially in sexual inter-
course. Such communication demands honesty and a giving spirit to
plumb the depths of joy.

It's hard to keep communication consistent with commitment. It
tends to lag behind or run ahead. The latter is especially true of sexual
expression. Because our sexual appetites are the most clamorous of
our physical longings, we risk plunging into relationships without
regard for long-range consequences.

If one climbs the high board with intent to dive one must be sure
that there is water in the pool. Likewise, before we enter into expres-
sions of intimacy, we need to be sure that the relationship has integrity
and rests on responsible commitments.

God made such a marvelous creature when he made a human being
that it takes more than a lifetime to know him or her. We continue
to explore each other's thoughts, values, loyalties, the things that
concern us.

In all human living, rhythm is essential. In marriage too, it is necessary
to the health of a relationship to draw apart as well as to come together. Neither party must over-possess the other.

Wouldn't it be simple if we could live by a rule book? Imagine a
newly married couple sitting down at their new kitchen table and saying, "O.K., let's work out our rules, six for you and six for me"—or
"six hundred for you and six hundred for me," and living by a check
list for the rest of their lives. But the trouble is that they are in love.
They must live through all of the future in the healthy fear that they
are not everything to each other that this relationship requires or per-
mits. The demands of love reach farther than the demands of law.

Love is never satisfied. Notice how people in love behave: they observe each other's every word and gesture, they explore each implication and attitude. Love's favorite language is the question. Love reads. Love listens. Attention is its first gift.

"It is a fearful thing to fall into the hands of the living God" (Hebrews 10:31), scripture tells us. We have thought of this mostly in terms of God's wrath and just vengeance against us for our misdeeds. But what if it applies more to the claims upon us of God's love? Like living in marriage, to live in this love relationship is a joyful but fearful thing. Brooding over one's days is the fear that one may disappoint the beloved and be untrue to love's vast dimensions.

—*Portions adapted from "Hungers of the Heart"*
  and "These Things I Remember"

Words at a Wedding

We cherish for you
joy and peace in believing,
the joy of trusting
and of being trusted,
of forgiving
and of being forgiven.

We cherish for you
the enriching rhythm
of togetherness and separateness,
for unless you are at home in the soul's stillness,
you cannot be God's intention
to each other.

We cherish for you
the rhythm of silence and loving speech,
for relationship is tested
by how it employs silence
amid the many forms of speech.

We cherish for you
the rhythm of privacy and intimacy,
that you may not over-possess each other,
for before you yet knew each other,
you belonged to God.

We cherish for you
the rhythm of pain and pleasure.
We speak not now of inevitable pain,
but of the pain you choose because you care,
for "without a hurt the heart is hollow."

We look with longing after you
but run with hope before you.
In the bittersweet joy of your departing
we pray:
God bless you unto more and more
of living and loving.

—*from "A Second Look"*

Things Too Tall

I remember some things that were too tall for me. In fact, this memory is not only mine but yours as well.

Do you remember when you lifted your hands to face level to wash and then were told not to spill on the floor? Do you recall how, by the simple operation of the law of gravity, the water ran down your forearms and dropped from your elbows because the washbasin was so high?

Do you remember what it was like to stand on tiptoe and reach for something on a table only to have it fall on the top of your head? Or do you recall with me the experience of drinking from a water fountain, when it was purely by chance that any water reached your thirsty throat, yet it was a certainty that in the process your face would be drenched and your clothes too?

Do you remember standing in a forest of knees and thighs and seeing only feet and trousers and dresses when you accompanied your parents in a crowd? Or do you recall sitting in a gathering and being told not to fidget when your feet dangled eight inches from the floor?

One of my most dramatic memories, when I think about things that seemed very tall, is of dogs. Do you remember how big the dogs were?

But why recall these small frustrations? Maybe because they were not little to us then and are not small to our children today. It may help us to make a more concerted effort to enter into the world of children and understand and respect them. Let us who are adults remember that children are people, and that we should not turn them into toys but rather recognize the dignity of each little individual and take seriously his hopes and fears, her triumphs and tragedies.

—*from "These Things I Remember"*

The Home: Laboratory of Love

The home is a great laboratory for testing the power of faith and love. God's benediction rests over the unpublished words and unheralded acts of those who make our houses into homes.

We are born into a network of umbilical cords. The doctor is in control of the first. But from there on are other dependencies and interdependencies which must be carefully guided and regulated. These require faith and hope—and much love.

In almost every family there are sharp differences in the members. Some are confident and socially at ease. Others may be slower to find their place and release their gifts. Some are competitive and assertive, while others need special support lest their gifts be stifled and their development impaired.

Adults can be humbled by the sincerity and forthrightness of children, who haven't yet learned the pernicious arts of evasion and camouflage. To expose oneself to the unselfconscious naturalness and sincerity of children can be enlightening, even when it embarrasses us to death.

When our son John was about three years old, he already had a great interest in cars. He and I were driving down the street one day when a very handsome car pulled alongside ours, and John said, 'What kind of car is that?" And I said, "That, John, is a Cadillac." And then he said, without any hesitation, "When can we get our Cadillac?" What he didn't know was that we had hardly paid for the hubcaps on our Chevrolet. But I was complimented—even if a little embarrassed—because he opened the door to his trust. It told me what he thought of me.

We influence each other for good when we enjoy. Parents shape their children most decisively, not when they scold or correct them, although at times this is necessary, but when they enjoy them. Even after the nest is empty and the adult children come home for visits with Mother and Dad, this enjoyment doesn't lessen.

Love and law are not opposed to one another. In the best homes love makes itself known even in the tensest situations. It is the one great constant under all conditions. It makes the home a haven to which family members may come when they feel defeated and a harbor from which they leave for new explorations and experiences.

Most of us appreciate the familiar things in our search for stability. We are entertained by novelty, but we are nourished and sustained by stability. At every age, wherever we go, we need someone and somewhere to return to.

We want a rock to stand on. As parents, our responsibility is to provide bearings and directions, a point of reference for our children in their little and larger journeyings. All through life the best part of every journey should be the joy of coming home.

To see a child disappearing into an adult is awesome. Our children and grandchildren seem to grow up when we have our backs turned.

One of the wistful times for a parent is the moment of realizing that the child is no longer a child. She has "left the nest." He has "flown the coop." We have been disqualified for directing or correcting. They have outgrown us!

"How quickly they grow tall," we say. Deep in our hearts is a wish to freeze the river. We want to stop the flow of time. Our need to be needed can over-assert itself, and we may struggle to keep the child in our world. It is especially hard to admit that some of our children's ideas and insights are better than our own. One of the most difficult of the arts of parenting is to receive our children's mature gifts without defensiveness or resentment.

Our young people rise to challenge and to judge the false goals which we have pursued. They indict us, not necessarily for our failures, but for the emptiness of many of the prizes we have won. They smell the smoke that rises from the fires of our hatreds and hostilities.

When our generation feels a chasm away from our children, grandchildren, and other youth, we may wonder what we can do. Perhaps we could best concentrate on being someone to them and less on *doing*. We owe our young people an example of steady, habitual gratitude.

We can do nothing greater than to wear a path to God's presence and our brothers' and sisters' need. Our children will not always walk with us, but they will see the path. And in time they may set forth on it.

Little ones need someone to run to, but so do big ones. Parents who pray give their children an enduring gift—the gift of One to whom we may always run.

—*Portions adapted from "You Are Blessed" and "Hungers of the Heart"*

God's Family: The Church

"There is one body and one Spirit, just as you were called to the one hope of your calling; one Lord, one faith, one baptism, one God and Father of all, who is above all and through all and in all" (Ephesians 4:4-6).

Neither you nor I can read the secret thoughts and hopes of our brothers and sisters in the faith, but one thing we know, and that is that we look up to the same cross and name the same Christ. We are "called to the one hope."

When God justifies us in Christ, we are given an identity and need no longer struggle for a name. We belong.

But we do not exist for ourselves. We find ourselves in relation to others in the community of faith, the Body of Christ. To grow in our relation to Christ is to enter more and more fully into God's purpose for us and to celebrate our oneness with other believers.

"'Tis but as men draw nigh to thee, my Lord,/They can draw nigh each other and not hurt" are words of the poet George Macdonald. They express the hard fact that unless we are in the company of Christ we are not safe company for one another.

Imagine a body in which the fingers scratch at the eyes and the mouth bites the hand. One member warring against another is repulsive.

How many of us have not shared the childhood disappointment over the thought that Jesus went away and is now way up there when we wish that he had stayed down here. But our Savior ascended into heaven, not to draw way from any one of us, but to draw closer to all of us. Like the spokes of a wheel, you and I are closest to each other when we are close to the center, our Lord, whose body we are.

There were two little brothers named Nicholas and Casey. When Casey was born Nicholas was about four years old. A month or so after Casey's birth, Nicholas said to his grandma out of the blue: "It's hard to be big brother." And she asked, "Why, Nicholas?" And Nicholas said, "Well, every time Casey cries I've got to go and say, 'There, there.'"

Now you and I know that that's hard work. If we don't understand that, there's no use explaining it. But what are we here for? We're here to say, "There, there." Casey doesn't understand one "there," two "theres." But Casey understands presence: voice, touch, embrace.

What is the church? Is it a great company of debaters and explainers? No, the church is a place of embrace, of presence, of voice, of touch.

Not long ago I heard a friend say that we speak too often about the poverty of the Christian church and too seldom about its riches. He was right. We do talk a lot about the petty motives and evident hypocrisies of Christians. We spend ourselves in whipping ourselves and others, wallowing in guilt, while we should be running the glad errands of the free.

Lifestyles vary in the Christian community, patterns of service differ widely, but these variations do not signify disunity where Christ is king. Perhaps no generation of Christians has been called upon to accept and rejoice in as many different ways of expressing the Christian hope as we who live now. Congregations do not have to be divided because of sharp differences of opinions if they will recognize that deep unity that exists when people share the same hope.

There is ample room for disagreement within the Christian commitment. God does not intend that every member of the family shall think alike. Where everyone thinks alike no one thinks very much.

When God's people differ, they can nevertheless respect each other and be mutually enriched as they share their talents. When differences are not cherished and respected, the entire community is impoverished and God's purpose is hindered.

The phrase "one body and one Spirit" is heavy with divine possibilities. It invites us to enter into our true humanity and share the joy of believing. When we see one another through our Lord, we can rejoice in each other's gifts and share our common life. Then we can also feel each other's hurts and respond to each other's loneliness and anguish.

—Portions from "What in the World Are We Doing?"

God's Family: The World

"Live in harmony" is God's command and challenge to his family on earth. But there can be no rich harmony without a loving and creative com-bination of differences. Beauty and richness express themselves through variety. God's artistry in nature utilizes an unlimited variety of shapes, colors, smells, tastes, textures, and sounds. He never repeats a snowflake or a sunset. But God's supreme art is in his creation of persons.

In God's world, as in the church, we need each other's differences. We need to rejoice in them, since no one takes the place of another. Christ would heal our divisions and draw all people of every color and country together, creating his own rich harmonies in the midst of an infinitely vari-ous humanity. In Christ, God gives us to each other. Let us receive his gift.

Whoever I am, I am another of God's originals, unduplicated and unique. No one in this multicolored mass of human beings combines exactly the same capacities and characteristics as I. No one is intended or equipped to play just the same note in humanity's symphony.

Because I am a servant of Christ, all people who are in any kind of need have a right to me. If I am a teacher, the ignorant have a right to my knowledge. If I am a doctor, the sick have a right to my skill. If I am strong, the weak have a right to my strength.

The church sometimes walks with timid heart and lagging steps. Its tasks are left undone while it turns in upon itself. So much of our program of evangelization is really a beating of the bushes for people just like us, peo-ple who think as we do, live as we do, and look like we do. The poor are often forgotten, the disgraced are avoided, the strangers are shunned. Interracial inequities and injustices continue to fester in our society. Love and understanding falter, and our concerns are feeble and unexpressed. The arm of compassion hangs weakly at our side.

We even try to find religious reasons for turning away from brothers and sisters in distress. They are not of our faith, we say, and we must care for our own. And so we try to use Christ as a wall instead of letting him be a bridge. But our common humanity places a claim on us all. We are meant to receive and accept our sisters and brothers in the spirit of Christ, who has accepted us all.

Our great wealth as a nation becomes either a wonderful means of express-ing life or a tragic way of demonstrating a condition of stagnation and corruption. Material things in themselves are not bad, but kept from those in need, they become the very caskets that shelter the selfish in their living death.

On the playground unhappy children scatter because no one can win the argument and everyone wants to be first. In the community the task remains undone because someone else may get the credit. In the state and nation poverty and hunger go unassuaged because of competitive self-interest. On the international scene, the desire for lordship leaves the conference table vacant while young men bleed on battlefields and mothers weep. Hopes are deferred and hearts sickened for lack of cooperation and goodwill.

Even in the small moments of day-to-day living we can feel helpless in the face of things we can't understand, wrongs we can't correct, events we can do nothing about. How much better off the world would be if we all had more compassion, and could better understand the dark and difficult moods of ourselves and others!

"People are so mean these days," a gas station attendant said to me the other day.

"Why do you say that?" I asked.

"Just because," he answered. "They think it's all my fault. You know —the price of gasoline."

Each of us needs practice in walking in our brothers' and sisters' shoes, in seeing things from another perspective. We need to learn to condemn less and understand more, to reject less and accept more.

And who are my brothers and sisters? Who are not? Where is the foreigner if this is my Father's world? Where am I a stranger? Where am I not at home? Which war is not a civil war? Where is the problem that is not a family problem? Should I speak of home and foreign missions? Should I not rather think and speak of family missions?

*—Portions from "Homing in the Presence"
and "A Savior, a Song and a Star"*

They Bring Us Up

Wet-cheeked and defiant,
he made his last-ditch stand:
"Are you going to be
the kind of mother who forgets
that her child is only
five years old?"

And she, his mother,
caught in the classic net
of parenthood, was held at bay—
no, vanquished, as love and wisdom
met surprise.

The little children lead us.
They search us with their invincible innocence,
stir wells of cleansing memory
and raise new springs of hope.
They restore our lost perspective;
they bring us up.

STRUGGLING

All Over Again

It was a quiet lane,
one of the many in that Wisconsin wood
at the spacious retreat ground
where we were staying,
my friend and I.

We walked and talked,
for our friendship
went back to school days,
and here we were,
past middle age.
The swift years had brought gifts,
as they always do,
of memorable joys
and chastening sorrows.

We had married at about the same time,
but after very few years
his wife had died.
We spoke of that, and I said,
"You've been places
where I haven't been.
You've learned things
that I can't really know."
"Yes," he said, "but one has to learn them
all over again!"

His words checked me then
and have disturbed me since.
Perhaps this is the significance of sorrow,
that it underscores and rehearses
great meanings, so that,
in the round of daily experiences,
we do not lose them.

—*from "Bless My Growing"*

Grandma's Quilts

I remember Grandma.

I remember the black kerchief she wore around her head tied in a bow under her chin and the broad-brimmed hat on summer days when she went berry picking along the fence lines or in the woods. I recall her profound loyalty to her own language and the customs of her mother country, the dollar that usually accompanied her Christmas greeting to each of us, the peppermint candy and the words of commendation on occasions when I had learned my catechism lesson well. I remember too her fierce prejudice against cats, especially when she was feeding our favorite dog. I remember her hymnbook and her Bible. I recall Grandma's unschooled common sense and her humble faith in God. But most of all I remember her patchwork quilts.

Grandma's quilts were a source of fascination to me, especially on days when we couldn't go outside because of the weather. It was fun to watch her strategy unfold into beauty as she worked on her patchwork quilts. There were many scraps and threads, each a vivid color. I would watch and wait to see which color she would choose for each particular patch. Sometimes she would let the choice be mine. My favorite pieces of all were the squares of black velvet she interspersed judiciously among the colored ones. These served to highlight her bright floral decorations and embroidery.

From the underside, however, the patterns of the patchwork quilts were far from beautiful. They seemed confusing and senseless. As I think of this, I remember the daily providence of God. He is not a sadistic devil who enjoys seeing his child suffer. But in the context of his purpose to rescue us he does permit some sufferings and tests to touch our lives. Viewed from our side, the underside, his plan is often confusing, and we are tempted in our darker moments to contradict it.

There is beauty in the patchwork quilt of the Christian life. It has its dark hues, but its brighter colors are glorified in contrast. God's purpose is unfailing. When we are tempted to charge his order with being disorder and to want our own design, of this we can remind ourselves: though there is mystery in evil, there is also mystery in the good.

—*Adapted from "These Things I Remember"*

Grounds for Hope

If I am asked
what are my grounds for hope,
this is my answer.

Light is lord over darkness,
truth is lord over falsehood,
life is ever lord over death.

Of all the facts I daily live with,
there's none more comforting
than this: If I have two rooms,
one dark, the other light,
and I open the door between them,
the dark room becomes lighter
without the light one
becoming darker. I know
this is no headline,
but it's a marvelous footnote.
And God comforts me in that.

—*from "A Second Look"*

After You Have Suffered

"After you have suffered a little while, the God of all grace, who has called you to his eternal glory in Christ, will himself restore, support, strengthen, and establish you" (1 Peter 5:10).

"After you have suffered"—I read these words and I don't like them. I see something in my path, and I want to fly over it, burrow under it, detour around it, anything but go through it. Here I encounter the ongoing battle with each human will, the challenge to affirm life rather than renounce it, to advance rather than to retreat.

When we are singled out for something pleasant, we see this as a gift. But when we seem singled out for pain, we may cower and demand, "Why me?"

Patterns of stress change. Circumstances of testing come to all but in different ways. No one among us knows exactly how or where or when we will be put to the test, but for every one of us "the hour is coming."

The storms of life are impartial. They strike all people. It may seem to us that some are comparatively untested. The life of another often looks easy. But there are no untested lives.

Suffering is not out on the edge of life. It is at the very center. It is the very stuff from which God makes meaning.

Life itself is a painful but wonderful gift. It is not meant to be lived by me on my own strength. It is not a human-sized gift to be managed by human powers. It is a God-sized gift to be lived by God through each person, precious in the sight of Christ.

He who is trustworthy inhabits our pain. He lives in our fear and forsakenness. With his hand over ours, we dare to answer life's summons. We find courage for discipleship and are surprised by the joy too deep for words.

God's gifts of salvation and hope are given to all his children, yet remain personally and privately ours. "Why me?" we might well ask about his gifts.

The suffering is for "a little while." The glory is for always.

—*Portions from "Silent Spaces"*

Waiting

It is the last day of August, and the summer has been one long sea-son of almost unbroken heat. The forests seem to cry for life as the trees drop their leaves several weeks earlier than usual in defense against their very death. Many of the usual woodland flowers are hardly visible, and all the little moving creatures seem to be in a state of mourning. An unhealthy silence settles over the land, and the mood of waiting is upon us all. We wait for water. We look for the rains that don't come.

One of the most difficult of life's assignments is to wait. The life of faith is one of working and/or waiting. We all know that it is easier to work than to wait. Times do come, however, when all we can do is to hold still and wait.

In every life there must be two kinds of power, the power to act and the power to endure. The bridge and the locomotive are both necessary if cargo is to be carried across the river, the active power of the locomotive to pull the load and the passive power of the bridge to bear the weight.

Faith allows us to take Christ at his word when he says, "Come" and when he says, "Go." It helps us to work when conditions are right for working and to wait without bitterness when waiting is all that we can do.

This day may find you homebound. Perhaps you have experienced surgery. Or maybe you're in a discouraging stage of a long illness. Or you may be resting after a flare-up of a chronic condition, something you've been told you'll "just have to live with."

Are there hours of weeping in the night, moments of bleakness and forsakenness in which you lose your assurance that you really are held in God's grace and cherished forever? Whatever your situation, know that he is active for good in your life, even when you can do nothing that the world considers important.

This is what we are here for, to strengthen one another, to shout encouragement through the storm.

Waiting for visible healing, suffering ourselves or on behalf of loved ones, we sense that our only hope is the fact that Jesus walks through all the doors that are closed to us. His love moves with authority where we cannot go.

I know a place where the traffic is heavy, and faster than sound or light. Although it is intimately personal and very private, I can't understand it. It is the traffic in my own mind. I am sometimes frightened by it because it runs away with me. It is most troublesome when time hangs heavy on my hands because of illness or forced inactivity. Many "what ifs" threaten to rob me of my courage and kill my joy.

In the midst of this, these words come with healing and help: "You are not lacking in any spiritual gift as you wait for the revealing of our Lord Jesus Christ. He will will also strengthen you to the end, so that you may be blameless on the day of our Lord . . ." (1 Corinthians 1:7-8).

We hold the promise that God does not hold our past over us, or use anything that we are or have done against us. Neither the evil we have done nor the good we have failed to do can destroy us. Christ has done his work. It is finished.

What, then, shall we do with ourselves meanwhile? Shall we scold ourselves in self-disgust? No, rather, let's ask our Lord for a comforting sense of humor. He knows what it's like to be human.

Seeing the absurdities and oddities in life, and especially learning to laugh at oneself, can lighten many a burden. Laughter has been called "internal jogging." When our bodies no longer consent to physical jogging, why not use our abundant opportunities for internal play and exercise for those situations to which we can find a funny side?

Quiet weather is building weather. Today, if you are not in pain, if you sense little turbulence and turmoil within, use the time for living and loving, reflecting and thanking, being and doing, believing and receiving.

Build well now by inviting Jesus to take charge. He is both carpenter and storm stiller.

But if you are in pain, if your suffering seems more than you can bear and you are ready to say, "It is too late; there is no hope for me," look to Jesus again. Let him take command of the storm. There is no need to suffer the destruction of all that is good and precious in you. God has not placed it there to be lost.

We must wait, but we need not wait in suspense. We need not wait as convicted murderers await execution. Living as we do in the joy of "all things accomplished" but also in the pain of "not yet," we wait in hope without losing courage or sinking into despair. We may wait as children wait to be let in on a festive party. To wait with eager longing can become our greatest strength.

The grace-formed life is heaven's art. Let the Spirit work. The Spirit will shape your life and mine into beauty and strength and will sustain us in every storm.

—*Portions from "Silent Spaces" and "Deep in December"*

A Child's Scream

I remember the day I heard my child scream in pain.

It was a warm August day in 1952. Our four-year-old had complained of a headache and was also a bit feverish. We were not disturbed at first because these symptoms are common to children. However, on about the third day we noticed that she began to swing her hip as she walked. I shall never forget the chill that ran through me as I first thought the word *polio*.

An examination by our family doctor indicated that a spinal tap was required. He arranged an appointment at the local hospital. We tried not to telegraph our anxiety to the little one, but we must have been unsuccessful, because as we neared our destination, she said, "I guess I'll just sit in the car."

I shall not forget being ushered into an emergency room where there was a long table. The doctor called me aside and said, "You will have to hold her firmly because a spinal tap is painful."

In a matter of minutes I found myself bending over the child and holding her hands much tighter than a father wants to hold the hands of his four-year-old. As I leaned over her, she screamed into my ear,
"I told you that I just wanted to sit in the car!"

I have often thought in later years how many times I have screamed these words into the ear of God. The time comes to all of us when love takes us by the hand and leads us to the place of pain. These are moments when we plead for exemption and immunity from the suffering to which our broken race is heir. But love is too wise and kind to let the beloved exchange present pain for ultimate injury.

So it was for my daughter: surgeries and long hours of physical therapy would take her from wheelchair, through crutches and braces, to walking on her own again.

Soon or late, in my life and yours, God makes of us spiritual astronauts. We are of the fellowship that prays, "Thy will be done." By this we volunteer for more than a walk in the garden or even a ride in a car. God can send us instead on a moon shot. We had better be dressed in our space suits when we pray this prayer, for it is not at all pedestrian. Joyful adventures, but sometimes with painful struggle, come to those whom love can't let "just sit in the car."

—Adapted from "These Things I Remember."

Comfort My People

Our time is marked by a tragic loss of nerve. The panic button beckons, and we find no confidence by looking into the faces of the crowds. We try to comfort ourselves by hurrying a little faster or studying a little harder, by being "up-and-doing," but we hardly know which way is up or what is worth doing.

In our preoccupation with everything from measles to arthritis, we skirt our main problem, which is our sin. The authority of medicines and prescriptions receives more attention and veneration than the God against whom we have sinned.

Suffering in the agony of Satan's if: "If you are the Son of God . . ." With us, the adversary uses another attack: "If you are a child of God . . ." "If there even is a God . . ." "If God loves you . . ." The list is endless. It is an ancient strategy.

Hell's seedsman looks for soil in which to plant his poisonous weed of doubt. He is patient; he only asks for soil and root room. He will water the seed and keep it shrouded in darkness, for unbelief is a night growth.

"Comfort, comfort my people, says your God. Speak tenderly to Jerusalem, and cry to her that she has served her term, that her penalty is paid, that she has received from the Lord's hand double for all her sins" (Isaiah 40:1-2).

"If you had only recognized on this day the things that make for peace!" (Luke 19:42). Our Lord's voice choked with tears as He spoke these words over Jerusalem, "the city of Peace," the city that belied its name.

Proud in the midst of privilege, rebellious in the face of responsibility, careless of peril and opportunity alike, Jerusalem refused to repent.

Jerusalem did not have the sense to weep for herself. So Jesus wept for her. With the perceptiveness of perfect love, Jesus saw that this city was at war with herself. He saw the one thing that could keep this city alive and make her people great—the mercy of God.

For us, the citizens of Jerusalem, life is not simple or serene. We still find ourselves caught in the complexities of trying to live with one another without betraying our trust as human beings.

A great preacher, Joseph Parker, said, "There is nothing which a man in grief dreads so much as uncomforting comfort; he cannot bear to be spoken to by those who do not know what comfort really is."

Any comfort that does not speak to our guilt and our sin against God is "uncomforting comfort." But the comfort of the gospel awakens us to the best and greatest resource we have; namely, the mercy of God, which frees us for a new life. Consciousness of such a treasure rouses us and lifts us out of despair.

The poet George Macdonald speaks of life's pains and troubles as the sharp-toothed sheepdogs that the Good Shepherd uses to drive us back when we wander and to keep us close to him.

It helps to consider the wounds of Christ when our own burdens choke back our praise and our sorrows drown our doxologies. When the sheepdogs nip at us and send us to the shelter of the Good Shepherd's presence, they are the disciplines of God's caring love and saving purpose.

We need a larger screen upon which to view our little lives. We need to sense that God is in our history and nothing can separate us from his love. Like sheep looking to their shepherd and daring to graze because he is near, we dare to give ourselves to the day nearest at hand, living one day at a time, because our confidence is not in our own brain or brawn but in him. We believe that we are loved and cherished. We know our Shepherd stands beyond our farthest vision even as he comes to us in the present moment. This we believe because he has shown his face in the face and tears of Jesus.

Creatures Great and Small

My dad was a Danish immigrant, a carpenter when he came from Denmark, and when I knew him, a country preacher and farmer. We had a cow we called Dagros. She was red and white, the matriarch in our small herd.

I recall most vividly the time that she became sick and lay suffering for several days. The best knowledge of the neighboring farmers and of a competent veterinarian was not sufficient, and her condition became progressively worse.

An annual mission festival was being held at our church. I told one of the missionaries, a kindly and sympathetic man, about our sick Dagros. He walked with me to the pasture. When he saw this suffering creature, he took a leafy branch and gently brushed the flies from her head. He stood there and said, *"Ja, at mennesker skulke plages, det kan jeg godt forstaa, men ikke at dyr skulde plages."* ("Yes, that people should suffer, this I can well understand, but not that animals should suffer.")

Today I saw a dog, a pitiful, deserted dog. He looked as if it were a great mistake that he was born. He had no friend. He seemed so beaten and broken. He slunk along in fear and forsakenness.

The suffering and the neglected animals who populate our world stir a thorny doubt in my mind, a doubt that has often beset me and robbed me of my pleasure. I've wondered, like our visiting missionary of years ago, what sense there is in a world where such things can happen to a cow or a dog or any other of the creatures in our care.

I meet here a profound mystery, a problem that I have never solved. How can it be that the nonmoral element in creation shares the suffering of fallen sinners like you and me? Certainly here lies a hint of the basic kinship of all living things.

Life lives on life: the lower forms serve the higher, and the higher serve the highest. We do not know why animals experience pain, but surely it should cause us to approach them in reverence and deal with them in a humane and gentle spirit. Even in the business of farming we are to cherish and nurture life—life in the seed, life in the egg, life in the womb, life wherever it is.

I cannot answer my own questions, but I do find comfort and light in scripture. "Are not two sparrows sold for a penny? Yet not one of them will fall to the ground apart from your Father. And even the hairs of your head are all counted" (Matthew 10:29-30). This has something to say to both the great and the small among God's creatures. It guarantees that God is not indifferent.

The whole creation groans and waits, waits because even now God is working out his plan. I can't answer my own questions, but I can turn my face toward him and believe that God will somehow, in his time and in his way, acknowledge and honor every work of his hand.

—*Portions from "These Things I Remember"*

The Cup

Yes, Father, it does run over,
it really does. The cup, I mean.
But God, I didn't know, I couldn't guess
how big the cup would be,
how much of pain, but more of joy,
it someday would contain.

I'm glad today, and thankful too,
for that early blindness. For had I seen
what fills it to the brim,
I would have spurned the cup.
I wouldn't have dared touch cup to lip.

I offer now my tear-stained praise.

—*from "Kept Moments"*

Amazing Grace

"I really don't think that I'm a better person
than I was when I was twelve years old."

Words of truth and wisdom from my friend,
a man of more than seventy years,
a mellow and insightful person.
My heart speaks thanks on my behalf,
for this is my self-appraisal too.
We may grow in openness and understanding,
be kinder, gentler, more accepting,
but never be less in need of grace
and never problem-free.

Maturity—What is it, really?

Perhaps it is this, and much, much more:
to cease expecting ease and tranquility,
to learn to navigate in sunshine, storm, and fog,
to know there are no hideaways where one
escapes oneself
and leaves one's problems far behind;
to realize that no good thing is ever cheap,
that most of life is bittersweet
and comes as crisis, calling, challenge.

—*from "A Second Look"*

An Enemy Has Done This

A child dying of third-degree burns in a hospital ward, a father weeping over a lifeless form lying by the roadside, a family walking in the rubble left in the wake of a tornado, a woman staring vacantly hour after hour in a state of mental derangement and brokenness. Everywhere sorrow and anguish, disorder and confusion, and over it all a brooding, tormenting mystery, and the tortured question, "Why?"

What can we say in the face of true tragedy? The will of God? God's way of punishing? Heaven's way of keeping us humble? Trials for our training? No, rather let us say as Jesus does in a parable, "An enemy has done this" (Matthew 13:28).

A few years ago a college student named Greg was bringing a sailboat into shore on a windy day when the tip of the mast touched the high line. He was instantly electrocuted. I was called to come to Greg's home. It was many blocks away, but as I drove I wished it were farther. I had no answers for that situation.

When I came to the door the boy's mother and aunt, whom I knew well, met me. And I knew of nothing else to do but throw my arms around them and say, "I come not with wisdom but with love."

Stand on any corner of a busy street and view the burdens people carry, burdens that some have carried since birth and others since some tragic event. Then look again and read their faces, their walks, their postures, and you will see deeper. Look once more and reflect. Think of all that is hidden. Look into your own being and be reminded of all that is secret; the fears, the searing dreads, the dark misgivings. Over all of this, the same thing must be said, "An enemy has done this."

This is not the way our loving God intends his people to live. This twisted, distorted world is not according to God's good pleasure. God uses suffering but it is not his will; he takes no pleasure in the sorrows of his child.

Every person experiences the desert, that place where there is no hope in human resources. Tidings come, and all the news is bad. Perhaps it is disease that is the problem, and every doctor is helpless. Days become weeks, and week after week there is no change for the better.

Hopes are dashed and night sets in on the desert. Or perhaps it is not a matter of physical pain and sickness, but rather of psychic desolation and emotional weariness.

The last enemy is death. My life and yours is lived "in the valley of the shadow of death." But God is no stranger here.

"Was it not necessary that the Messiah should suffer these things?" (Luke 24:26).

For this heaven-sent sufferer it was not just a few terrible hours on one hellish day. It was suffering all the way, the suffering which poverty, rejection, shame and guilt inflicted on this sinless One. It had to be even more than this. It had to be the very God-forsakenness of Good Friday.

It had to be. There was no other answer to our human plight, no answer either in human individuals or in committees or in conventions of people. We had no hidden reserve to draw on. No human trick or act of heroism could heal our break with God.

"My God, my God, why have you forsaken me?" (Matt. 27:46).

This cry is not the snarling profanity of a grounded spirit, a man cursing his circumstances. It is not the guttural groan of one who is crucified on consequences. This is the cry out of hell by the One who did not deserve to be there!

Why was Christ forsaken? In order that no one on earth need ever be a God-forsaken person, in order that no place on earth need be a God-forsaken place, in order that no moment in time need be a God-forsaken moment.

Without the fact of our suffering elder brother, all is tortuous nonsense, and I cannot endure it. But because God himself has entered into the whole world's anguish and into my most private sorrow, I can go on.

Our Secret

"May the God of hope fill you with all joy and peace in believing, so that you may abound in hope by the power of the Holy Spirit" (Romans 15:13).

Once in a while one person among many may act differently in a given situation because he or she knows a secret. The secret of the Christian is hope. It is really no secret at all because it makes itself known through love. Only the person who lives in hope is free to love.

To struggle is one thing, but it is quite another to struggle without hope. To suffer is hard, but to suffer without hope is unbearable. Hopelessness is meaninglessness. Without the secret, nothing holds together.

Our savior came to be our hope. He asks us to live in the open secret as we love and support one another. Of all the gifts that God holds in store for us, we can trust him to preserve the gift of hope, for it is the very heart of his plan and purpose.

When the Word became flesh, the great miracle occurred. All that happened in Christ's ministry is but the inevitable result of the incarnation, the event by which the Almighty One visited us.

Faith's response to Love's command is still the way of miracle. When Jesus' mother said at the marriage at Cana, "Do whatever he tells you" (John 2:5), she put the secret into words. Wherever and whenever we meet Christ and risk obedience, there something happens— God's "something." There blessings pour forth like rain from the clouds. This is the breakthrough that makes sinners into saints. To believe is to give God right-of-way through one's life. It is to trust in him and to let him manifest his glory in and through one's self.

When we live in hope led by the Spirit we live in the dawn. We experience life as more and more. Even though the body grows tired and its steps become less certain, the inner life is richer and the spiritual light shines brighter. The big things become bigger, and life becomes more focused so that one is less distracted by trinkets or tyrannized by trifles. Love, joy, peace, and the other gifts of grace become enduring excitements that experience does not exhaust.

The Spirit-led person can look to the future because it belongs to God. Hope is many things, but above all it is freedom, for hope is born in forgiveness and sustained by love.

To live in hope is to accept one's future from God's hand. To abound in hope is to live in anticipation and expectation. It is to look forward to Christ's return with eager readiness, believing that all tomorrows are but the working out of God's gracious purpose.

Loneliest Moment

It happened one September morning
on a street in the Big Apple.
I shouldn't have been walking there.

With hardly a sound he came,
leaped across my path from nowhere
and pressed a long-bladed knife against my side,
His voice a whispered snarl:
"I want your money—all of it!"
With practiced stealth he robbed me
of my watch and all my cash.

I'll not forget the hostility in his eyes;
it was my loneliest moment.

But there have been other moments
when Truth has come at me
"from behind and in the night,"
when the long, sharp blade of fact
has blocked my path, leaving me no exit,
and stripping me of my pride.

The difference was in the face.
Truth is not foe but friend who comes
stealthily finding, capturing,
loving me into painful change,
stretching me in that lonely moment
into a larger becoming.

—*from "A Second Look"*

It's Yours, Lord

Forever—
I say it to myself, Lord,
say it again and again.
It frightens me. I'm tormented,
haunted, and all but upended.
It robs me of all peace and rest.

Forever—
too long, too deep, too high,
too much, Lord.
I can't handle it.
You take it please.
It's yours, all yours.
You hold it, and me,
in the hollow of your hand.

—from "Kept Moments"

Glimpsing Glory

"Six days later, Jesus took with him Peter and James and John, and led them up a high mountain apart, by themselves. And he was transfigured before them" (Mark 9:2).

"Then a cloud overshadowed them, and from the cloud there came a voice, 'This is my Son, the Beloved; listen to him!'" (Mark 9:7).

There are high mountains in the life of every believer, moments that make a significant difference and do not leave one the same. God gives times of unexpected breakthrough, experiences that light lamps for the dark valleys of human existence. Our temptation at such times is to try to cling to the feeling of such a moment rather than to its meaning. Peter, recalling the transfiguration experience, later referred to himself and his companions as "eyewitnesses of his majesty" (2 Peter 1:16).

Have you ever experienced a strange change of mood in the midst of distress, a change that you just can't account for, because circumstances haven't really changed that much, or even at all? Have you had a sense of well-being and felt a caring love envelope you? I have. And I interpret this to be angels come to minister to me. I believe it is the miracle of God's healing love.

I remember a day that comes to everyone, the kind full of discouragement and disappointment. I found myself in a rancid mood. It was worship time on our campus, and even as a teacher I went reluctantly and unexpectantly. I felt defiant and discouraged. As one of my friends arose to bring the message, I inwardly challenged him to say anything that would minister to my condition. And then, with his first word, it came: "Grace to you and peace!" Grace and peace—that was it, all I needed. Never have I felt the impact of these two words as I did that morning.

The Spirit brings the gift to me and shows me my name upon the gift. It is one thing to know that God is gracious to all; it is quite another to hear the words "to you."

But it is sobering to have our moment on the mountain. The disciples who were privileged to share the special vision on the Mount of Transfiguration found all of the nerve-tingling seconds sharpened into a terse command, "Listen to him!" Their new experience was to unplug their ears. They were left more exposed. More would be expected of them than before.

A contemporary Christian writer has remarked that after twenty years of struggling with his doubts, he has passed from the agony of questions he cannot answer to the agony of answers he cannot escape. But he expresses great relief.

I can remember when "the lights came on" for me when, as a young man, I first felt really gripped by God's loving intention and drawn into his plan. Since I have come to know Jesus Christ in a personal way, life has not been easy. It has not been sorrow-free. But it has never been empty. I have not been bored. The days have kept me looking forward, and life has been full of God's gracious surprises.

You and I may not have been granted such spectacular mountaintop visions as were witnessed by Peter, James, and John. But God has placed his signature of love upon our lives in many ways. He has given us glimpses of his majesty. It may have been in the joy over a well-born child. It may have been in a moment of sorrow and loss. It may have been something that caused us to catch our breath and respond in wonder and amazement. The Spirit works in many ways, but whatever the situation, it lets us say with Peter, "Lord, it is good for us to be here" (Mark 9:5).

HOMING

Aging: Trusting the Child in Us

It takes three extra words to describe me now: "for his age." "Isn't he doing well for his age?" It's scary.

My journey has been from the days when I hadn't had enough time to the days when I've had too much. "My, but he's eating well with a spoon for his age," they once said of me. They were charitable, compassionate. They knew that I hadn't had enough time.

Now I've had too much. I understand spots on an old man's neckties. It means he has to work harder to be presentable, because he eats with a trembling hand. And again he needs compassion.

I think of a "Peanuts" cartoon of years ago in which Linus has been waiting to get old enough to have a library card, and now he's old enough and has the card but doesn't dare go to the library. Charlie Brown, that benign little presence in his life, comforts him with: "Don't take it so hard, Linus. What you've got is 'library block.' Everybody's got some place where they're afraid to go." Linus asks, "What's yours?" And Charlie Brown says, "The world!"

In the old days they didn't varnish things as much as they do today. They talked often about the devil, the world, and our own flesh. These are a very unholy trinity that makes life scary, and if we don't see life that way, the chances are we don't see it in its reality.

We say, Father, Son and Holy Spirit. I think of God the Father in terms of human caring. I think of God the Son as one who is with us—"God with us." I think of God the Holy Spirit as the comforter, the fortifier, the one who stretches us but does not crush us, who does not break us but works carefully and tenderly with us.

We can affirm that the power behind this world is love, that the most satisfactory metaphor for our God is one who cares. That takes some of the scariness out of life.

I find life to be a journey from child to child again. It doesn't mean that you are to be childish, but it does mean that you must become increasingly childlike as you grow old.

We need to be childlike in our receiving. A child opening a gift doesn't say, "Oh, but you shouldn't have!" That lie is left to grown-ups. Small children won't say, "Can't I pay for it?" They have no buying power.

We live on gift or we don't live at all. Gift is the new content of the twice-born life.

A child lives within each of us, regardless of our age. And this part of ourselves must not be denied. For it is this child who rises up expectantly to follow, who trusts the Father's promise, who sits in Jesus' lap and finds there peace and comfort.

—*Portions from "Homing in the Presence"*

Aging's Best Gift: Today

She was 98 when I met her, and almost 101 when she died. I've been told that her eldest daughter was 81 at the time of her mother's death. That's a long time to be a mother in this bewildering world!

I wish I had asked my aged friend, "What is there, when one has lived as long as you, that is still more and more in this world of less and less?" I'm guessing she might have answered, "My people, my home, my Bible, my baptism, my prayer book, my hymnbook, and especially God's promise of eternal life." Perhaps her list wouldn't have been in that order, and maybe it would have been longer, but I'm sure it wouldn't have been shorter. She was a growing person until the very end.

When we prayed the Lord's Prayer together I was aware that she was leading me. She had lived her way more deeply into it than I. Hers was a longer history of gift. And she was grateful! She had learned the secret of living happily in this day.

There are oaks in the forests of God. They are gnarled and twisted because they have weathered bitter winds and stood against the harshest storms. But their very twisted and tortured look only adds to the rugged beauty that arrests the eye of beholders and elicits awe and respect.

These oaks are those trusting spirits who have stood firmly rooted in God's goodness and daily grace. They are the people who have been hurt by the years but whose hurt has only deepened their understanding and strengthened their love. They are those of whom the psalmist could say, "They are not afraid of evil tidings; their hearts are firm, secure in the Lord" (Psalm 112:7).

My maturity is tested whenever I'm asked to turn from myself and my preoccupation with my own needs to the problems of others. As a tiny tree becomes more than a tree on the day it offers habitat and shelter, so I begin to mature when I reach out to the weary and frightened around me who look for refuge and comfort in my company.

Life is not so much a matter of high moments as of common situations and numerous repetitions, calling for patience and unspectacular service. The lowlands and valleys are where each person is called upon to live. Even the most intrepid mountain climbers can't do their living on the tallest peaks. They must come down. But they can come with a memory of the sun on the glaciers, the vast vistas that were before them, and the breathtaking sights and sounds that surrounded them.

Life is not to be measured only by the number of years one has lived, but by the number of times one has caught one's breath or missed a heartbeat out of sheer wonder in the midst of God's gifts, by the lump-in-throat moments as one remembers the amazing faithfulness of God.

Winter brings beauties that are as piercing and profound as those of any other season. Its beauties are austere and moving. They are not so lush that they are distracting. They suggest depth and solitariness, encouraging meditation and introspection. Every path in the snow is clearly traced, and every birdcall or sound of wind and weather is carried over longer distances.

But winter's deepest beauty is the beauty of promise, especially the promise of another spring.

This is the day. God has made it. He has made it for you. To live in it is to begin all over again. It is to enter upon life's perpetual morning.

—Portions from "Deep in December" and "This Land of Leaving"

Homing in Presence

One day as I walked down the airport ramp to board a plane, a family of four was in front of me. The older child appeared to be about four and her every step was a bounce. She radiated expectancy and joy.

Her father looked down at her and asked, "Where are we going?"

"To Grandma's!" she shouted, punctuating her words with a higher bounce.

She didn't say "to Bismarck" or "Billings," but "to Grandma's." As far as she was concerned, she was going to a person—the place didn't matter. She was an eloquent witness to the fact that we home in those who love us, in people more than in places.

We seek to "home" in one another. It is meant to be so, even as we "home" in God, for he has given us to each other.

I am reminded of the fretful child who was asking for attention, and whose parent said: "Can't you watch TV?" And the little one said, "But it doesn't have a lap!"

As I remember lap time with my own little children, I remember that I received as much pleasure out of it as they did. You don't have to talk all the time. You immerse yourself in presence—you sense each other's breathing. The child senses the strength of the adult, I suppose, and finds it reassuring. The adult senses the trust of the child and finds that reassuring. I hope God gets that kind of pleasure when we come to him.

Last week, a letter came, telling me of the death of an old friend. We were college roommates for three years. Although I hadn't seen him for many years, his death reminded me of the thinning ranks of familiar faces in my circle of family and friends. Such thoughts cause one to reflect on life after death and on love's reunions.

I know little about death, but I affirm, with other believers, that in Christ love lives on, and nothing good is permanently lost.

Where are we going when we die? Everyone has the right to ask, but perhaps it's the wrong question. Rather, we would wonder, To whom am I going?

Again and again during his lifetime on earth, our Lord Christ said, "I go to my Father." To my father—to our Father.

We all want to unlock the deepest secrets of life and death. Jesus holds the key. When we make his words our own we hold the key to the future, the key that unlocks the last door.

—Portions from "Homing in the Presence," "This Land of Leaving" and "It Had Better Be True"

Free

Golden years they've had together,
a half century, plus five,
he of more than eighty Christmases,
she not far behind.

Today we met her as she walked alone;
she told us of his recent illness,
critical, but now abated.
She let us share her joy.

All through the hardest days
and darkest nights, she said,
she hardly broke her vigil,
and once, with tubes and needles
everywhere he woke to tell her,
"Nothing is bad when you are here."

Love's light burden,
more than law demands,
the golden binding of the willing heart
and ready hand.
These were her gifts of presence:
the smoothed pillow, the cooling cup,
the caressing touch, the loving voice
and smile of one so bound,
and yet so free.

—from "Deep in December"

My Bush Burned

My bush burned this morning,
burned and was not consumed,
as I gathered with sisters and brothers in the faith
for the ultimate act of defiance,
a Christian burial service.

My heart soared and sang
as I joined in the demonstration
and hurled the name of Jesus
into the face of the enemy,
Death.

Never have I sensed so deeply
the heaven-sent boldness
of comforting one another
"with the comfort with which we ourselves
are comforted by God"
and taking to the streets again
with other comforted ones
under the defiant benediction.

The bush still burns.

—*from "A Second Look"*

Homing in Promise

"I will come again and will take you to myself, so that where I am there you may be also" (John 14:3).

This is the voice of Emanuel, which means "God with us." It is the strong word of promise, made by him who stood ready to pay the price and deliver the gift. God loves us. God wants to be with us and to have us with him. We can even say that God misses us! He wants us "at home."

My middle name is Emanuel. I did not like that name as a child. I didn't think too much of Gerhard either, but Emanuel—that I kept secret all through grade school, high school and into college. I think I had a boy's hunch that it wouldn't "fly" on the playground or the sports fields. But today, as an old man, I draw great comfort from the name "Emanuel," especially because of certain experiences I've had with it.

One such experience was with a dear friend who had lung cancer. Sent home to die, she wanted her friends to visit her, and my wife and I came several times. One evening as we were leaving our friend said to me: "The next time you come we're going to talk about death."

She was a very discerning person, extremely challenging, so I prepared conscientiously to talk about death at our next visit. I read Romans, Thessalonians, and the 15th chapter of Corinthians. I thought through four or five approaches to death I hoped could help.

When our next visit came, I had an experience I'd never had before. I found I was like a child who had forgotten his piece. I couldn't think of a single thing except my middle name, "God with us." So that's what I gave my friend.

What do I really know about life? What do I know about death? I affirm that God is with me. "Emanuel" is the only reason I dare to grow old.

"And remember, I am with you always, to the end of the age" (Matthew 28:20).

"With you always." More than a thought, this is a fact. I circle round it, live my way into it, build my house upon it. It means that Christ inhabits my days as well as eternity, that he lives in my every experience, and I am never alone.

Truly, I tell you, today you will be with me in Paradise" (Luke 23:43).

There he is—your Christ and mine—between two thieves, just where he belongs, just where he wants to be, keeping bad company in order to make that company good!

Here is enough for everyone, enough love to come without invitation, enough grace to die without appreciation, enough humility to serve without honor, enough holiness to make all righteous, enough forgiveness for all sins, enough power for all weakness, enough truth to rout the darkest lie, enough life to conquer every death.

The Suffering Servant has visited our planet. He has walked the Home Road all the way from God to us, and he is the Home Road back to God, for he is love.

What did this mean to the forgiven one and what does it mean for you and me? It means that those who will may be free at last! It means release from the meaninglessness and misery of guilt and transgression, freedom from the pain of purposelessness and self-will. It means that we who are meant for goodness can be good, that we—like our fellow thief—can go hurrying home to our native air, to heaven and oneness with God.

There is someone in us who cries to be released. It is the one whom God intended you and me to be. I feel him within me in terms of errands of mercy never run, of words of encouragement never spoken, of letters never written, cathedrals never built, dreams never realized. You and I suffer the anguish of knowing that we are meant for greatness and are not great.

One day the persons you and I are meant to be will be fully released.

*—Portions from "A Savior, a Song and a Star"
and "These Things I Remember"*

Promise

April, and promise filled the air.
We sat beneath the oak trees,
retreating together and talking.
The subject: the right to live—
even when the road is uphill all the way
and only suffering seems to lie ahead.

One among us hadn't spoken.
Now he did—slowly, softly,
every word a painful effort;
"We mustn't deprive them
of the process," was all he said.

Did he mean that living,
even in its bleakest moment,
hold promise, promise like
an April morning?

Words to search and silence us.

—from "Kept Moments"

The Question

Today as we talked,
friend to friend,
she shared this memory with me.

Keeping vigil at her sister's side
with death only moments away,
she longed to share thought and feeling,
but the dear one had moved beyond,
out of reach as she lay
in comatose stillness.

Suddenly she stirred and startled the waiting one
with a question: "'Yea' what, Ethel?"
Some seconds of panic
("What does she mean? What does
she want? I mustn't fail her now!").
Then as a gift, the answer came:
"Yea, though I walk through the valley
of the shadow of death, I will fear
no evil, for thou art with me."

The dying one smiled and said,
"I will fear no evil, for thou art
with me, with me . . ." and on this
she pillowed her head.

—*from "Kept Moments"*

Mourning

Our telephone rang. The voice at the other end brought news of sudden death, the death of a father. Now we are thinking of our friend, an only daughter, devoted to her father. "How sad, and on Thanksgiving Day, too, just two hours before she arrived to celebrate this festive day. It's going to be hard for her as she looks into the years ahead."

To grieve for someone is to pay a great compliment to that person. It is to ascribe meaning and significance to that person's life. It recognizes the importance of community and is a confession that one can't be human alone.

In a world where death takes no holiday, what is there for the one who looks ahead through tear-filmed eyes?

All around me I see and hear the heavy footfalls of death. I witness change. Faces wrinkle, footsteps falter, canes and crutches become life supports.

Death and bereavement meet us everywhere, on the country road or in the busiest shopping mall. Hidden in many a smile is a tear, the shy longing that waits for a word well spoken. Our calling is clear. The Comforter makes comforters of us so that no person need be lost in the crowd.

What can we say in a cemetery? What can be said that tombstones and caskets cannot contradict? Surely, this is not the place for quick and easy speech. Even our best wisdom is an impertinence if the words are only ours.

I recall the funeral of a friend. It happened that not only was he my classmate but he shared my birthday. Because of this coincidence, I felt very dramatically the significance of the Christian burial service. I saw it as a beautiful act of defiance in the face of the enemy, death. I drank in the meaning of each promise in the scriptures and rejoiced in every stanza of the hymns.

When we rose to receive God's benediction I asked myself, "Why do we stand?" Then answered my own question: Because there is more traveling to do.

Is there a new word, a true word, a glad word that will not fail in the face of death? There is. It is the Word: Jesus. "He is going ahead of you" (Mark 16:7).

This fortifies me for the time when death will claim someone whom I hold dear. That will be the moment for going on.

Two roads will beckon, the road of isolation and the harder road of fellowship with others. I will be tempted to retreat into my sorrow, and I will need God's saving grace to help me to reach out my hand to my sisters and brothers. And as I do, I believe that God will meet me there.

This world is God's, and we are guests in it. Every moment moves us toward the day of freedom and fulfillment. We are a forward-looking people. As members of the body of Christ, we lift our eyes and sing our way into the changes that must come. In spite of present pain and doubt, we affirm our conviction that God is God, and he keeps his word.

Let the changes come. The future is God's, and he will give it as a gift to us as we receive his grace through each swiftly passing day.

The trumpet belongs in the cemetery, not for taps but for reveille.

—Portions from "Hungers of the Heart" and "It Had Better Be True"

Confronting Our Own Death

All of us spend some time—some more, some less—in contemplating death. We have to; we are all dying.

Death is real for each of us. It can't be bought or bullied, coaxed or frightened. It is there. No clever cosmetics can cope with it.

Like most people, I am arrested from time to time by the thought of death and eternity. I recognize such times as the stirrings of God's Spirit at my heart's door. In earlier years I thought most often of other peoples' deaths and seldom of my own. In later years, however, I am consciously under God's searchlight, sometimes in seclusion and sometimes in the fellowship of others.

"Anxiety is inevitable. . . . Don't make it worse by deceiving yourself and acting as if you were immune to inner trepidation. God does not ask you not to feel anxious but to trust him no matter how you feel."

These words from the pen of the late Thomas Merton help me to be honest in dealing with my fears.

I used to speak of making friends with one's dying hour. Today I will not say this. Death is our enemy, the last enemy to be encountered.

Someone had to come who could tower over death and command it. Someone had truly to enter into it who could break its power by rising again. But it had to be real death, no sham battle, no counterfeit experience. And so Christ came to die. This was his errand. It was as the archenemy of death that Jesus died so that we might be with him forever.

Jesus breaks trail into the unknown. His mercy lights the path through the years ahead and through the moment of dying. His mercy is the path.

I remember two words spoken in the stillness of a hospital room.

A note left in the church office summoned me to a local hospital. A young mother had lain for some weeks succumbing to a dread disease. I had administered Word and Sacrament to her there many times.

For twelve hours now she had not spoken or seemed to recognize anyone and appeared to be in a coma. There seemed only a slight possibility of getting through to her. However, I bent over the patient and slowly spoke several passages from Scripture. To my amazement, she roused herself and spoke two words: "Repeat them."

In her extremity this child of God did not ask conversation with fellow persons. She sought it with God.

We needn't faint with fear if we know who and whose we are.

Jesus died for me. And now I dare to face the dark fact of my personal death. I'll say it till I die: "Lord, I believe. Help my unbelief."

We will always be surrounded by gentle reminders of our mortality: the march of the seasons, the changing colors and falling leaves. Whether we are young or old, our times are in God's hands, and we are wise to leave them there.

—Portions adapted from "It Had Better Be True" and "These Things I Remember"

The Gift

1927.
Well I remember the long winter
and days of tired waiting.
I was seventeen
at home with my sister, six,
while Mother kept bedside vigil as our father's life slowly and painfully
ebbed away.

Hard days,
today a memory, but more
of the giving of the great gift.

He'd given much, and now,
mind and spirit weary,
body spent and broken,
one thing remained: a thought,
for me a life-directing gift.

I wasn't there;
he wouldn't have known me;
he knew no human face,
not even hers, my mother said.

He couldn't find words
to speak his crying needs;
yet two remained:
"Praeke evangeliet! Praeke evangeliet!"
Hour after hour, day after day,
in that, his final week:
"Preach the gospel! Preach the gospel!"

Blessed residue,
two words, one thought,
expressive of the habit
of one spent life—
to us the last, the best,
the greatest gift.

—from "Blessed Is the Ordinary"

Homing in Eternity

Death has been called the moment of supreme clarification. Because our Lord is the Light of the world, it is consistent with the life of faith to think of death in this way.

"See, the home of God is among mortals. He will dwell with them as their God; they will be his peoples, and God himself will be with them; he will wipe every tear from their eyes. Death will be no more" (Revelation 21:3-4).

No more death! Bolder words cannot be spoken. No more parting. No mournful procession to the silent city on the hill. No haunting realization that the last enemy must still be met. No wistful backward glance or anxious forward look. No pain at sunset or fear at dawn.

"I saw no temple in the city, for its temple is the Lord God the Almighty and the Lamb. And the city has no need of sun or moon to shine on it, for the glory of God is its light, and its lamp is the Lamb" (Revelation 21:22-23).

In the new kingdom of the saved, we will experience life in new dimensions. We are lost in wonder when we try to reflect on the fact that even the sun and moon will have fulfilled their purpose and no longer be needed. It steadies us to rest in God's unchanging love and care and to know that grace will reign supreme in every "then" and "there."

One of the meanings of John's vision is that God will lift back the veil of his created world and meet us face to face. It is impossible for us to take this in.

C. S. Lewis put God's assurance this way: "At present we are outside of the world, the wrong side of the door. We discern the freshness and purity of the morning, but they do not make us fresh and pure. We cannot mingle with the splendors we see. But all the leaves of the New Testament are rustling with the rumor that it will not always be so. Some day, God willing, we shall get in."

We cannot lift back or cut through the veil that hides the specific details of life beyond the grave. But we believe in the risen One and entrust to him our resurrection.

God's face is toward me. Beyond my most anxious moments lies that moment when all clouds will vanish and I shall see him. Then all his purposes will be clear.

—*Portions from "Hungers of the Heart"*

Takk for Alt

She was not quite 97
when she died.
One who waited at her side
heard her say it:
"Takk for alt"—"Thank you for everything."
It was her home-going word to God.

Like a good guest
she addressed her Host.
She spoke as one well-taught,
well-taught by life,
by memory and expectation.

To be gift-conscious is to be wise;
to know whom to thank is grace indeed.
To know the gift and love the Giver,
to have learned life's dearest lesson,
is to be rich toward God.

—from "Bless My Growing"

Acknowledgments

As noted within the text of *Journey of the Heart*, excerpts are reprinted from the following works by Gerhard E. Frost:

Chapel Time, copyright © 1956 Augsburg Publishing House.

These Things I Remember, copyright © 1963 Augsburg Publishing House.

Bless My Growing, copyright © 1974 Augsburg Publishing House.

Homing in the Presence, copyright © 1978 Gerhard E. Frost. Reprinted by permission of HarperCollins Publishers, Inc.

Blessed Is the Ordinary, copyright © 1980 Gerhard E. Frost. Reprinted by permission of Ivern Frost.

Kept Moments, copyright © 1982 Gerhard E. Frost. Reprinted by permission of Ivern Frost.

A Second Look, copyright © 1985 Gerhard E. Frost. Reprinted by permission of Ivern Frost.

Hungers of the Heart, It Had Better Be True, Deep in December, You Are Blessed, Silent Spaces, and *This Land of Leaving* (*God's Way for Me*), copyright © 1986 Logos Art Productions. Reprinted by permission.

What in the World Are We Doing?, copyright © 1987 Logos Art Productions. Reprinted by permission.

A Savior, a Song and a Star, copyright © 1945 The Board of Education and the Young People's Luther League of the Evangelical Lutheran Church. Reprinted by permission.

Excerpts are reprinted by permission of the Shepherd Company from the following un-bylined bulletin cover meditations written by Gerhard Frost during 1962-1976:

R-76104 ("Introduction: Journeying"); R-7361 & -7213 ("Roses in Winter"); 1022 and R-6882, -7524 & -7672 ("God's Longing"); 1007 & 1011 and R-7142 & -7333 ("Journeying Through Prayer"); 1001, 1010-1012, 1014-1017, 1010-1012, 1017 & 1021 and R-7274 ("The Perfect Prayer"); 1018 and R-6873, -7565 & -73103 ("Christ's Question"); 7291 and R-7113, -7474 & -64121 ("Our Secret"); R-7114, -7623 & -67111 ("Lord, I Believe"); R-6751, -6865, -6942, -7062 & -7381 ("After You Have Suffered"); M-6531 and R-6584, -7283, -69102, -72123 & -72122 ("Comfort My People"); R-7564 ("Creatures Great and Small"); R-43, -1033, -7321, -7542 & -7573 ("An Enemy Has Done This").

Also: R-3122, -7521 & -73121 ("Looking with a Child's Eyes"); R-7053 & -7253 ("Opening to Surprise"); R-42, -6543, -6811, -6941, -7023, -7323, -7395, -7532, -7753, -7514, -7614 & -73102 ("Follow Me"); R-67123, -69122, -71122, -73123, & -74123 ("Blessed Is He"); M-6533 & -6564 and R-6812, -6985, -7051, -7324, -7563, -7714, -67113 & -71104 ("Go and Do"); -6455 & -7173 and R-6413, -6423, -6814, -6852, -7055, -7155 & -7421 ("Do Love"); R-7622 ("Rhythm and Relating"); R-7024 & -7693 ("Marriage . . ."); R-6954, -7094 & -7271 ("The Home . . ."); R-6921, -7012, -7294, -7362, -7414, -7471, & -7551 ("God's Family: The Church"); 7191 and R-6864, -6984, -63125 & -68103 ("God's Family: The World").

Also: R-6572, -6972, -7391, -7431 & -70122 ("Judge Not"); 7214, M-6561 and R-6813, -7164, -7492, -7591 & -71111 ("Forgive and Forgive"); R-7094, -7274, -7413 & -70121 ("Give Thanks"); R-6952, -6953, -7344, -7534, -7535, -7763, -66122 & -73124 ("We Are Witnesses"); R-6842, -6952, -7431 & -67102 ("Share the Party"); 7223 and K-6764 and R-6791, -7092, -7361, -7543, & -66113 ("Time"); 7185 and R-6871, -7561, -7743, -67103 & -72101 ("Waiting"); 1009 and M-6734 and R-7372, -7432 & -7522 ("Aging's Best Gift: Today"); R-7142, -7454, -7533, -72113 & -76114 ("Mourning"); 1036 and R-7263 & -7434 ("Confronting Our Own Death"); R-41, -6961, -7022, -7544, & -64123 ("Homing in Promise"); M-6561 and R-7063, -7452 & -7453 ("Homing in Eternity").